Scenes from la Cuenca de Los Angeles

y otros Natural Disasters

Other Books

by Susana Chávez-Silverman

Tropicalizations: Transcultural Representations of Latinidad,
coedited with Frances R. Aparicio
(1997)

Reading and Writing the Ambiente: Queer Sexualities in Latino,
Latin American, and Spanish Culture,
coedited with Librada Hernández
(2000)

Killer Crónicas: Bilingual Memories
(2004)

Scenes from la Cuenca de Los Angeles y otros Natural Disasters

Susana

Chávez-Silverman

The University of Wisconsin Press

Publication of this volume has been made possible, in part, through support from POMONA COLLEGE.

The University of Wisconsin Press
1930 Monroe Street, 3rd Floor
Madison, Wisconsin 53711-2059
uwpress.wisc.edu

3 Henrietta Street
London WCE 8LU, England
eurospanbookstore.com

1   3   5   4   2

Printed in the United States of America

Library of Congress Cataloging-in-Publication Data
Chávez-Silverman, Susana.
Scenes from la Cuenca de Los Angeles y otros natural disasters /
Susana Chávez-Silverman.
p.   cm.—(Writing in Latinidad: autobiographical voices of U.S. Latinos/as)
Written in a combination of English and Spanish.
ISBN 978-0-299-23524-6 (pbk.: alk. paper)
ISBN 978-0-299-23523-9 (e-book)
1. Chávez-Silverman, Susana.
2. Latin Americans—United States—Biography.
I. Title.   II. Series: Writing in Latinidad.
E184.S75C485   2010
973′.00468—dc22
[B]
2009040632

Para Pierre

Dicen que la distancia es el olvido,
pero yo no concibo esa razón.
Roberto Cantoral (Mexican composer),
"La barca"

Contents

Contents

Foreword

Paul Saint-Amour, University of Pennsylvania

For when was light a public thing? It surely lies instead as reclamation lies, in the empty space of each completed sentence, which lets grammar muse upon some possible nights it could have spent with grace. Darkness, after all, is too literal a hiding-space, pretending as it does to make a secret of the body: since secrecy annuls, eats up, what is significant in surface, it cannot be sufficient to our tastes.

Sara Suleri, *Meatless Days*

Shedding darkness, encrypting through publicity. For the writer, such a daylit veiling has a clear and powerful appeal: a chance to shape the life and self that are disclosed and the contours of what stays withheld. But how does the reader of such a complex offering draw near to it? What would it mean to accept an invitation like the one extended by Susana Chávez-Silverman's new book?

Scenes from la Cuenca de Los Angeles y otros Natural Disasters is crisscrossed by intimacies. These crónicas are curved toward their dedicatees, and most of them harbor moments of direct address, often in friendship's private argot. As readers we must enter at speed into stories that are already underway, upon places and recollections where the writer and addressee seem to have dwelled together for years. "That luxury hotel." "Those lion-colored hills de ambos lados de la 280N." Even the demonstrative adjectives are heavy with a shared history that is likely strange to us. "Ese slow-as-lodo SEPTA commuter train que nos regresaba de Philly a un rainy y *mega*-stuck-up Princeton." And in a departure from its predecessor, the present book includes transcriptions from the author's diaries, sharpening the impression that we are listening in on confidences meant for other ears, or for none. Such a book might leave its readers feeling at once untimely and intrusive, like latecomers to an eavesdropping.

How is it, then, that so many have responded to Susana Chávez-Silverman's work by saying they felt called by it, chosen by it, emboldened and consoled by it as if it were speaking directly to them? This address happens in many voices, shifting not only between Spanish and English but among dozens of registers and inflected localities in each language. Likewise with cultural references: this is writing that swerves from Cortázar to *Cat People* in a few sentences, dashes laterally from Louis Malle to Frédéric Malle. The energy with which the work refers and travels, toggles and relates—this would seem to guarantee virtually any reader at least a few moments of connection. Yet flexibility and range alone cannot explain the sense that we have been welcome from the start within the work's radius of intimacy. We get closer to that welcome by recognizing that, for Chávez-Silverman, conjuring an addressee is not an optional way to constrain her readership but a condition of expression, a necessity. In the opening pages of *Killer Crónicas: Bilingual Memories* (2004) she tells us, "I can't write sin sentir el latido del corazón (or at least el tecleo de manos on a keyboard), las pulsaciones cerebrales—verbales—de un interlocutor." The nearest interlocutor is often a particular crónica's dedicatee, but that figure's most important role may be to serve as the reader's onstage representative, the Horatio through whom we receive confidences without trespass. These confidences are angled subtly toward us through a pedagogy of friendship that says: Here are the means—the shorthands and coinages and commemorations—by which intimacy might speak; and, what's more, they may be learned. To traverse Chávez-Silverman's writing is to learn to speak as her close friends do, so that one can no longer do without "chévere" or "órale" or "feliz" or "cacademic" or "ternura" or "anygüey." Even "San Francisco Transcript/Diary," the present book's most concave space of self-communion, bears this epigraph from Irene Vilar: "Distance is a proposition that points to an audience besides yourself. Distance is a book." Vilar's words end with writing's distance, but their point is proximity: it is only through the distance of a book that the reader may be brought near.

Many of the crónicas in *Scenes from la Cuenca de Los Angeles y otros Natural Disasters* read as if they had been composed at a single sitting, with a purity of impulse that wanted no revision. "I can't not write it like I hear it," the author has said. But one would have to add that she takes the trouble to listen more than once. For while it's true that Chávez-Silverman drafts in fervent bursts, her work is also meticulously refined and revisited. Seven of the crónicas in this book first appeared in literary and scholarly journals; others made their debuts at public readings. To compare earlier with later versions is to see these pieces at once unfolding within and musing upon a field of alternatives. A minor example: one early draft of "I Want the Wrapper Crónica" contains the phrase "no tengo las respuestas a estas (ni, for that matter, a casi ninguna otra) preguntas, OB-vio." In a later version, this becomes "I don't really have answers for these questions. Ni, for that matter, a casi ninguna otra." Such substitutions, slight in isolation, are extended to the level of a practice in this book, in whose chosen words and phrases one can hear the unchosen codes ghosting like an overtone series, in every "question" a phantom "pregunta." In the aggregate, these branching choices open out on something larger: the other itineraries that a life, lived in many places and through many codes, might have taken. Here is grammar musing upon some possible nights it could have spent with grace.

The counterfactual the life unled but unforgotten—is one of this book's deepest preoccupations. At its heart is the author's reconnection with a former lover, a white South African: as she rereads her diaries from their time together, the mountain retreat where she is staying becomes a "memory vortex" in which the past returns with almost no loss of resolution or intensity. Almost no loss; but also absolute loss. Because we do not only live with our intimates; we also curate experience with them. When a lover goes out of your life it's as if that collaborative exhibit had burned. And when you conceive and lose a child together, as they did, that child is knit up in all the lost experiences of the life once shared. No wonder those two lives, lost together, are also recalled together, first through the diaries and then through the author's renewed correspondence with Howard. That exchange confirms for her that she does not remember or mourn alone, and that her decision not to stay with him was strong in that it led to the future she now richly inhabits, a future in which it is possible to write of not having stayed. Nonetheless, heeding the call of the forgone leads to a haunting query: What if I had, after all, been able to emplot a future with him in that country, at that time? This counterfactual question, in which memory and imagination and eros fuse, is unsettling, but not only that. It is reparative, too, asking as it does how things would have been if history—if *this* history—had not intervened.

Killer Crónicas opened with an account of writing as requiring "las pulsaciones cerebrales—verbales—de un interlocutor." *Scenes from la Cuenca de Los Angeles y otros Natural Disasters* amplifies a claim that was already, if more quietly, present in the earlier book: *memory*, too, is intersubjective. Memory, for Susana Chávez-Silverman, entails an addressee; it always begins with a name in the vocative case. One way of accepting the invitation of this book (there are others) is to receive, yes, but also to reciprocate its second-person address. This is a book to call "you" in the reading of it—not because we mistake it for a person or because we acquiesce to all of its demands, but because we recognize in it a writing unafraid to be partially legible and intermittently disclosive, a writing that understands both yielding and resistance as crucial forms of the accompaniment it seeks. "Stay with me a little while," says its opening invocation to blossoms, musos, reader; let's seek "más strange familiars." Your singular entreaty to tarry, stay, abide.

Acknowledgments

For their support of me and my writing, often via the increasingly quaint—según algunos—medium of e-mail (no he caído presa todavía al Facebook, or CaraBobo, como le digo, pero never say never . . .), I thank the following friends and colleagues: José Cartagena-Calderón, Lucía Guerra, Andrea "Chabelita" Gutiérrez, Daniel "el Itch" Hernández, Shaun Levin, Jorge Mariscal, Alistair McCartney, Tim Miller, E. Miguel Muñoz, Andrea "Silvana" Ostrov, Chris Sadiq, Tina Schiller, Ana María Shua, Ilan Stavans, Adam Teicholz, Miguel Tinker Salas, Paulina Vinderman, Suzinn "Lee" Weiss, Pamela Williams, Joanna M. Woolfolk, and, *in memoriam,* Howard T. Young.

The help of my research assistants—Jonathan Raz, Elaine McGlaughlin, Bethany-Rachel Bentley, and Marian Williams—has been invaluable. Para Uds., my heartfelt thanks. I am especially grateful to "el J-Raz" for designing the book cover and to Bethany, "la B," upon whose keen bilingual and creative writing–trained eye I relied during my "brief yoke"—the months of opposition entre Saturno y Mercurio during which she and I revised this manuscript.

Slightly different versions of various crónicas appeared in the following journals, and are reprinted here with permission: "In My Country Crónica" and "Unos Cuantos Piquetitos Crónica," *When Pressed* 2, "Movement in Language" (May 2009), http://whenpressed.net/collections/editors/movement-in-language/; "Diary Inside/Color Local Crónica," *PORTAL Journal of Multidisciplinary International Studies* 6, no. 1 (January 2009); "Arañita Cobriza Crónica," "Trincheras Crónica," and "Hawk Call Crónica," *SLAB (Sound & Literary Art Book)* 3 (May 2008): 21–23, 42–44, 120–23; "Currawong Crónica," *Chroma: A Queer Literary and Arts Journal* 6 (Spring 2007): 46–48; "Oda a la Ambigüedad Crónica," *PORTAL Journal of Multidisciplinary International Studies* 3, no. 2 (September 2006).

I've performed different versions of these crónicas in many venues during the past four years. Mil gracias to the following friends and colegas for indulging my Sagittarius-rising penchant for far-flung locales as well as my Moon-in-Leo embrace of the spotlight: Melanie Nicholson (Bard College, Annandale-on-Hudson, NY, September 2004), Paulina Vinderman and Martha Goldin (Biblioteca Nacional, Buenos Aires, Argentina, October 2004), Adriana Estill (Carleton College, Northfield, MN, February 2005), Eva Valle (University of Redlands, Redlands, CA, March 2005), Florence Moorhead-Rosenberg (Boise State University, March 2005), Azila "Tzili" Reisenberger (University of Cape Town, South Africa, August 2005), Edward James Olmos (9th Annual Los Angeles Latino Book & Family Festival, October 2005), David William Foster and Elizabeth R. Horan (Arizona State University, Tempe, April 2006), Alicia Gaspar de Alba (University of California, Los Angeles, June 2006), Paul Allatson (University of Technology, Sydney, Australia, July 2006), Emilie Bergmann (University of California, Berkeley, September 2006), Conrad Romo (The Hotel Café, Hollywood, CA, September 2006), Ray "Raimundo" and Terri Riojas (Square West Gallery, Pomona, CA, November 2006), Juan Poblete (University of California, Santa Cruz, November 2006), Carol Dell'Amico (California State University, Bakersfield, February 2007), John Carlos Rowe (University of Southern California, Los Angeles, March 2007), Tom Callinan (Rio Hondo College, Whittier, CA, April 2007), Sergio "Serge" de la Mora, Robert McKee Irwin, and Desirée "la Desire" Martín (University of California, Davis, May 2007), Darrell B. Lockhart (Biblioteca Nacional, Buenos Aires, Argentina, July 2007), Rebecca Morgan (Valdosta State University, Valdosta, GA, October 2007), Juan Carlos Galeano (Florida State University, Tallahassee, October 2007), Deb Cohen (Slippery Rock University, Slippery Rock, PA, October 2007), Verónica Dantán (Allegheny College, Meadville, PA, October 2007), Lázaro Lima (Bryn Mawr College, Bryn Mawr, PA, October 2007), Carlota Caulfield and Héctor M. Cavallari (Mills College, Oakland, CA, February 2008), Adelaida López-Mejía and Robert R. Ellis (Occidental College, Los Angeles, CA, February 2008), Laura "Lauris" Gutiérrez (University of Arizona, Tucson, March 2008), Elaine S. Brooks (University of New Orleans, New Orleans, LA, April 2008).

I owe a big debt of gratitude to the anonymous readers for the University of Wisconsin Press (I baptized you, together, my "ideal reader"), whose painstaking, probing, generous readings and suggestions pushed me to rethink, restructure, and rephrase. Also at the Press, eternal gratitude to my dear friend and longtime editor and Muso, Raphael Kadushin. To Chris Caldwell, *publicista extraordinario*, who pushed me way beyond my comfort zone in learning the art of the cold call (o, al menos, el cold e-mail) and urged me to "have book, will travel" during my recent sabbatical, mil gracias. Gratitude hasta la muerte to the ever-meticulous, cool-as-a-pepino Sheila Moermond, for her mega-editrixe skills. Thanks also to Carla Aspelmeier for her visual acumen, to Andrea Christofferson for her enthusiastic support, and to Scott Lenz, for translating me into sublime fonts, spaces, and ornamentos.

Pomona College's generous sabbatical leave policy enabled me to get far, far away from my *diario vivir* during 2007–8: in my mind and around the world. Most importantly, it allowed me to accept the artist-in-residency fellowship I was awarded by the Lucas Artists Program, for which I am very grateful. This residency renewed and transformed my life and my writing. I spent two sublime months in the Emerald Bosque, aka the Montalvo Arts Center in northern Califas. In that pristine, gorgeous retreat—at once familiar and unsettling—I finished writing this book.

My most profound gratitude and amor eterno to my Musos: Paul Allatson (a *special* ciberbeso transpacífico to you, darls, for your kicknalga formatting skills!), Raphael Kadushin, Wim Lindeque, Paul Saint-Amour, and Pablo "Hugo" Zambrano. And to Howard H. Geach, Muso *sine qua non* of this book.

Mil gracias a mis hermanas, Sarita "Eva" and Laura "Wiggue" Chávez Silverman, for always being there, for filling in my memory gaps (en palabras de César Vallejo: son pocos, pero *son* . . .), and for corroborating—and challenging—what I (think I) remember. A mi hijo, Etienne Joseph (aka Joey or el Juvenil), gracias. You're in here too. No demasiado (espero), pero you're here. Mi abuela, Eunice Van Wagner Chávez, passed away in July 2005, pero her spirit can be felt all throughout this book. She was my earliest model for a natural, playful, New Mexican Spanglish or code-switching, and I owe more to her loving ejemplo than I can possibly put into words, in any lengua. I want to remember here mis *muy* code-switching great aunt and uncle, Priscilla and Joe Rodríguez, who passed away, within two weeks of each other, in late 2008. And my cousin, their son Arthur Eli Rodríguez, drummer extraordinaire. Art passed away in October 2009. Q.E.P.D., queridos. Nos vemos on the other side.

Pierre, for your patience, love, laughter, uncompromising intelligence—for your presence—este libro se lo dedico a Ud.

Scenes from la Cuenca de Los Angeles

y otros Natural Disasters

Introduction

Cartografía Humana / Star Maps Crónica

12 abril 2009
Claremont, Califas

Yahrzeit, Brett Love, Q.E.P.D.

Aunque se dice que ignorance is bliss y también que curiosity killed the cat, hay que reconocer que a veces you *do* have to scratch an itch. So, en caso de que quieras adherir a este último dicho, this one's for you: un little road map pa' que luego, while you're reading, reconozcas a los principals en el cast of characters, la motley tripulación que me acompaña en este viaje-aventura called la vida.

Mi research assistant la Bethany-Rachel Bentley (avatar = Kristin Kreuk) es minúscula, hermosa y con un aura peculiarly estimulante y calmante a la vez. She's been with me desde su freshman year y está a punto de in-chickening herself en unas semanitas y no sé, te lo juro, qué será de mi writing, de mi vida, once she's hatched. Jonathan "el J-Raz" Raz (avatar = John Cusack, en los años '80) —former research assistant and unofficial advisee, hatched el año pasado y futuro architect ex Harvardis—designed el cover de este libro. Llevo cuatro años de intenso compinchismo, all around esta nuestra cuenca de Los Angeles, con este melancholic-jubiloso intellectual hunk.

Conocí a Paul "el Austra" Allatson (avatar = Guy Pearce) en el cyberspace, allá por 1998. La cosa fue así: el David Halperin me había mandado un essay to review, for la revista *GLQ: A Journal of Lesbian and Gay Studies*. Anónimo, OB-vio. Right from the get-go, tuve la sensación de estar ante la voz de un novísimo y desconocido pero fully formed, scarily brilliant Chicano scholar. El ensayo era sobre Luis Alfaro; era a la vez highly theoretical—citando a todos los de-rigueur intelectuales north and south and everywhere in between—y también vibrant, original. Sentí unas ganas locas de conocer al poseedor de esa voz—hasta un feeling of destiny—so I asked el David H. to hook me up. Fácil, dijo, he's an Australian doctoral student who lives just up the road from me.

Puf, up en un puff de humo went my latent, lurking raza-essentialisms: How *could* this Australian *oke* know so much, understand so much, *feel* so much about—and for—"my" cultura? Well, gente, ese y un sinfín de otros temas (rubros, como quien dice en la Argentina) llevo exploring—y explotando—con el Paulie these eleven years. Primero por e-mail, luego en mi casa, when he pitched up, sight unseen, en el 2000. He could be an axe murderer for all you know, refunfuñó mi pareja, who was quickly smitten cuando probó uno de los Indonesian curries que el Paulie whipped up, y vio cómo el Austra charmed al Juvenil, even lodged in the semi-rasquache and arguably too-close-for-comfort quarters del bottom bunk bed en el cuarto de un eleven-year-old. Anygüey, that was his first visit to the United States, to Califaztlán, región que sólo había conocido en libros and in dreams. Desde entonces, e-mails van y vienen, rendezvous en el norte (Madrith), Sur-ish (Puerto Rico, Miami, Los Angeles, Tucson) y al sur del Sur, en las mere mere antípodas, my girlhood dream come true at last: nuestro OZ-fest 2006.

Es el más crackshot investigador que conozco y tiene la más kick-nalga library on Latino studies, probably, en el mundo. Lee constante y vorazmente. Plus, he cooks a mean chicken to the oven, *and* whips up to-die-for sundowners. A tus pies, carnal, 4-ever.

Conocí a Wim "OomBie" Lindeque (avatar = John Malkovich) en 1983, en Pretoria. Me había separado de Howard, mi amor, y estaba en un all-time low. No tenía ningún sentido que estuviera living in South Africa si no estaba con Howard, pero como stubbornness and pride son dos de mis peores vicios, no way was I gonna turn tail y volver pa' Califas. Por suerte el Curé (aka Etienne Kapp, Q.E.P.D.) me había recogido, después de haberme abordado, on the street, with this incongruous greeting/pickup line: "Hey, you're not from around here, are you?" Me instaló en su apartamento en Sunnyside de un día para otro, y también, quick-quick, me instaló en su vida, heavily populated, in the main, with impossibly hip alterna-Afrikaners.

La noche que conocí a Wim, el Curé me llevó a una fiesta en casa del über-sexy W.A., un canchero indie-Afrikaner, alto, fornido y rubio, ostensiblemente straight, on whom *both* Wim and I had mega-crushes. No me acuerdo por qué, if it was some kind of fancy dress (aka costume) *partytjie* o qué, pero el Curé and I were wearing matching white karate suits. Con la diferencia de que mine was cut down *to there,* and cinched con un black obi. I had rubbed some chévere Stagelight opalescent powder (previously estrenado en el Limelight, en New York, so me sentía all that, wearing it to some little fiesta en Pretoria) into my décolletage. Me sentía bien insegura; the *only* person I knew remotely well era el Curé. Anygüey, el Wim me vino a saludar. Recuerdo que traía un atuendo eccéntrico, con muchos zippers. He was slim, and smoking, with a deep, sensual voice and perfect, gorgeous, PoCo South African English. Es decir, no hablaba con el típico acento de los Afrikaners cuando hablan inglés (which I would later come to find mildly endearing, pero sólo muuucho después . . .). I was enchanted. Pero what sealed the deal, según él lo recuerda, es que yo le dije: You are the *only* person here who's looked into my eyes—rather than at my busto—when talking to me!

We were inseparable after that, durante los casi tres años que viví en South Africa: desde las excursiones, every weekend, a Rocky Street (en Hillbrow, en Joburg) to *rooking* dagga (and risking una sentencia de por vida en las cárceles del apartheid, throw away la llave!), or dancing to live township jive en el Park Five Saloon, o bailando en conciertos de

Juluka en el Jabulani Stadium en Soweto, where we got in, no problem, porque el OomBie entonces trabajaba de—agárrate—*polisie.*

Yebo, a *long* ways from disaffected, bisexual '80s club-kid and too intelligent para ser *EngelsBoer* policía to politicized, passionate Catholic priest, viviendo y trabajando en Manenberg, a coloured township, uno de los parishes más pobres en Suid-Afrika. EYE: todavía le gusta la ropa. Ya no esos zippered getups, OB-vio (it was the '80s; what can I say?). Prefiere los cashmere sweaters que yo le compro on sale en Lands' End.

Nuestro bond—resucitado first by letters, then e-mail, luego en mi retorno a South Africa en el 2005, y lately nourished in his annual summer treks to Califas—es por vida. Aquí, allá. En el ciberespacio, en los frustratingly one-way textuals (SMS's, as you call them)—que yo puedo mandar y tú recibir, pero not vice versa—*in ons harte.*

I met Paul Saint-Amour (avatar = Keanu Reeves), aka el Santo-Amor (or Dr. Holy Love, as baptized by Wim), cuando nos pusieron juntos en el Teaching Committee en Pomona College, en 1999. At the time, él sospechaba que yo tenía un little colega-crush on someone *else* en ese comité, pero nothing más lejos de la verdad. The truth is, from the very first moment I caught a glimpse of that shock of black, black Hapa Momo–hair, and found myself on the receiving end de ese thoughtful, conspiratorial, blazingly brilliant gaze almendrado, I was a goner. OJO: I *was* kinda wary of him. Había escuchado los campus chismes de que P.S.A. era una especie de wunderkind. The top candidate in English en *todo* el país, fíjate, the year he went on the job market, según un amigo. Plus, I used to see him, for a couple of years hasta conocerlo en la carne, walking across the quad—con ese su particular bouncy, casi-Tigger walk—in the company of this rather obtuse y bien stuck up then-colega que mejor shall remain nameless (pero cuyo apodo era "Bert 'n' Ernie"). So anygüey, operaba una especie de fixation and disavowal a la vez (*pace* Lacan).

Hasta que un día—por algún oscuro motivo sólo explicable por la proximidad de Uranus a mi moon in Leo en la eighth house (or maybe it's Neptune?)—I went boiling into his office, intuyendo, somehow, a sympathetic ear, a safe space, a pesar de su rep as an intellectual heavy. Comencé a contarle some tale of woe and, to my horror, de repente I began bawling my head off. Allí delante de ese boy genius, aloof (so I'd thought), cool-as-a-cuke double Virgo. Por poco me morí de ver-güenza. Supe después que he is actually galvanized, siente una atracción empática, in fact, hacia mí. Hacia mis lágrimas. Hacia mi corazón. *And* to my writing, to the words con que canalizo y represento mi demasiado-squishy corazón. El Santo-Amor had stifled his *own* lá-grimas, repentinamente, a los diez años (por una über-pérdida, pero esa es otra) y tuvo que re-aprender a llorar (he told me this years later) ya de adulto y a duras penas. Appearances can be deceiving: actually, he has no problem at all con las lágrimas ajenas. Al contrario. Y desde esa tarde in his office nos hicimos fast friends. Tu decampment para Penn, Paul, is still an open wound, pero we have our words, we have our selves— textuales, elípticos. I read you; I transmit myself to you not nearly enough in shared glances, or laughter, or martini or Rémy-sips en estos días, alas, but it will have to do. Estos haikulike shards, voice messages, e-mails imploring, goading, brimming with confidencias, confesiones. You have my word(s): somos para siempre.

El que me hookeó con Pablo "Hugo" Zambrano (avatar = Eduardo Noriega) fue mi colega, amigo, mentor y Daddy-figura *sine qua non,* Howard T. Young (Q.E.P.D.), aka "el Joven" (avatar = Jeremy Planchas). That was waaay back in 1992. El Hugo had come to Claramonte ese verano para trabajar con el Joven, en algo renacentista, comparatista, something about poetry, OB-vio. Howard Young's expertise, tema ob-sesional de nosotros tres. No conocí al Hugo sino hasta el día antes de su departure, patrás a España. We met for dinner en un restó local y nos habremos dado como un mutual flechazo or something, pues we stayed there for hours, getting ever-loopier, tomando vino blanco until late en la sultry SoCal night.

Esa noche inauguramos uno de nuestros favorite games. We pick a cate-gory, say, kitchen parts, por ejemplo, y tenemos que decirlas in our weaker language para ese rubro. Mi educación arquitectónica doméstica was mos def en inglés, so es un huge thrill to be able to master words like mesada, bisagra, hornalla, grifo (canilla, en argentino), etc. Our biggest challenge to date, possibly, was finding the perfect rendition of "sleazy" en español. Not until Hugo was back in Spain, continuando nuestra apasionada si incipiente amistad by letter (quaint, ya lo sé!) y luego—we thought ourselves *so* sophisticated—por fax, decidimos que sleazy era "cutre."

Desde entonces, we've played our games parriba y pabajo, en mi casa en Claramonte y en la suya en Huelva. Coincidentally (o no), Hugo's star chart is uncannily similar to mine, ambos tenemos Grand Trine en fuego y el ascendente en sagitario. Traducción: we *love* to travel. Desde el épico road trip from Málaga to Ronda, comiendo habas con jamón roadside, en la ruta de los Pueblo Blancos de Andalucía, to the swampy streets de Buenos Aires en febrero—the *true* cruelest month—destornillándonos de risa con el strange léxico porteño and inventing faux traducciones like "egger" (for boludo), o llorando juntos, graveside, en el entierro de mi mamá en Santa Cruz, Califas, o ahora, hace tan sólo unas semanas weeping por teléfono, por e-mail, sobre la muerte de nuestro adorado Howard Joven: Hugo, estoy con voh forever, *fratello,* come what may.

Como siempre, la idea de la correspondencia, a connection—interlocutor, sparring partner, or love match—is paramount for my writing, for me (it is—yo soy—one and the same). Like in my last book, *Killer Crónicas,* like *The Mix Tapes,* que digamos, *The Mixquiahuala Letters* de la Ann Castle, or *Hopscotch,* de Julio Cortázar, estas crónicas constan de vignettes. Their genesis was in e-mails, cartas, diary entries, algunos refaccionados, como quien dice en Buenos Aires, otros somewhat more raw. They *do* tell a story, OJITO, pero not a (chrono)logical one. So if there's still a name or two que no reconozcas, between the acknowledgments y esta croniquita, si todavía estás confused, pos como quien dice en las clases de yoga: let it go. Just chill, gente. Go ahead and dip your toe into this passion/play.

Take a risk. Risk enchantment, como dijera mi carnal, el T. S. Eliot. Diviértete. Sobre todo, como dijera mi hairdresser y gran compinche el Ray "Raimundo" Riojas (avatar = Javier Bardem), just let yourself go. Allow the English (o el español: whichever lengua is most second-naturaleza to you, if you must—or can—choose) to keep pullin' you through. Ábrete, Sésamo.

You may have noticed que este little elenco carece de descripciones de algunos de mis *más* near 'n' dear. Well, eso es adrede, gente. Aunque quizás parezca que I bare my soul aquí en estas paginitas, por tener mi sol en la casa cuatro—ruled by hermetic, mysterious, privacy-protecting Cancer—en realidad I play my cartas *almost* as close to the chaleco as did my (Scorpio) mamá. So if you're still curious, pos Facebook 'em, háganles Google, baby! Y si por algún motivo you should come up empty handed, just use the best search engine ever invented: tu imaginación.

I

Diary Inside/
Color Local Crónica

23 junio 2008
Saratoga, Califas

Para los Musos: Paul Allatson, Raphael Kadushin, Wim
Lindeque, Paul Saint-Amour, and Pablo "Hugo" Zambrano,
in gratitude for your presence

Hmmm. Quizás abrir con algunos de mis diary entries. These fragments of "me." Mi instinto me dice que it's as good a way *in* as any, si bien un poco *in medias res* (pero quizás precisely *because* of this). Los diarios constituyen un modo más directo, a more *ostensibly* unmediated way (ja ja) to access, to convey la tremenda carga de intensidad, de recognition during these months here, en el Montalvo Arts Center. Desde el 3 de mayo I've been here. Simón, *yo. Me,* here. As an artist-in-residence. Put *that* in your pipa and fúmenlo, mijos. Pretty trippy, ¿qué no? Anygüey, el muñeco del Tim Miller me recomendó al Lucas Artists Program; I applied y fíjate que they picked me.

So heme aquí, amidst a somewhat motley crew of artists (mainly visual, hay que recalcar eso: soy, de hecho, la *única* writer-in-residence), residing en el no. 30 live-work studio (hagan Google al Montalvo Arts Center; "my" studio es el que sale como imagen emblemática on the website) en la parte residencial de la Villa Montalvo Arboretum.

Todo esto used to belong to James Duval Phelan, three-term mayor of San Francisco, financista y gran filántropo que también fue el dizque first popularly elected senador de Califas (1915–21). Lo que es realmente una intriguing (no) coincidencia, mejor dicho, una uncanny correspondencia: you know where el vato got the name Montalvo? Según me explicó mi colega y amigo José Cartagena-Calderón, el escritor español Garci Ordóñez de Montalvo, en su novela *Las sergas de Esplandian,* inventó una utopian island a la que puso el nombre de California. So en algún sentido, el Montalvo dreamed us, he *invented* us, carnales! Este Spanish Golden Age paraíso terrenal, poblado de amazonas y resguardado por griffins, tiene su correlato aquí, right here, donde estoy viviendo. José, siendo un erudito early modernist, o colonialihta, o transatlanticista, o como corno se les llame hoy en día a los antaño Golden Age scholars, recognized it immediately. Reconoció, I mean, its appropriately early modern, *literary* origins—cuando leyó la primerísima crónica que empollé y mandé desde northern Califas, a principios de mayo (it seems so long ago already . . .). Y allí me explicó toda la historia de Montalvo.

For me, este lugar ha sido un remoto y a la vez achingly familiar "green mansions," a memory vortex, lately turned, lamentablemente, terrarium. Me refiero a los record-breaking heat waves and eight hundred nearby wildfires y el concomitante smoke, ash, and singed, flying hojas de eucalipto, para ni mencionar a new batch of badgersome, heteronormativos, techno-geek resident artistes que llegaron en junio. Pero, ¿sabes qué? Ni modo. Soon I'll be leaving. Demasiado pronto. Isn't it *always* like that?

Dormí bien anoche, after two foreshortened nights. El viernes por la "ceremonia del fuego" en la slightly Wicker Man–esque summer solstice fest en casa de Luis Vásquez Gómez, un shaman-in-training amigo de mi hermana Sarita. Yeah, Friday was a weird, *way* too sultry, heat-blasted San Francisco night en la Mission district. Y anteanoche I stayed up real late en una slumber fest con mi carnalísimo, el Mexi–film studies scholar Sergio of the Berry. Esta mañana me levanté a las 7, el little white box ponía 60 grados y soplaba una leve brisa outside. Ay, alivio. The sky was strange and murky, though, y había un faint pero distinct olor a humo.

I carried la compu back up to la second-story loft, la torre, le digo (absolutely uninhabitable, por la falta de cross-ventilation, cuanto el mercurio rises above about 75 grados . . . how ridiculous, for a structure built to house a writer, ¿no?), con gran anticipación. Luego salí en el health walk, con mi Minolta. Había un chingo de annoying people en el lawn de la villa. Some adults, a gull of little kids. Es verano. Must be algún tipo de summer camp. Uf. Como que me estoy escapando justo a tiempo, it seems. Subí los so-called poet stairs. Qué poetas ni qué eight rooms, as el Sergio would say (en su still-tapatío even after décadas en San Francisco way): nalga-busters, *that's* what they are. The tilo trees donde comienza la escalera, sus florcitas, blooming and soapy-scented hace tan sólo tres semanas, now look kind of cowed, bien plain Jane. Las linden flowers disecaditas. Ditto the verga-trees. Los buckeyes. Their white-flowering phalluses flopping earthward ahora, cansados, scentless. No me gusta el verano.

Continué por el trail arriba, to the left of the stone staircase. Primera vez que lo hago all alone (ay, look how bold U R becoming, mija!). Quería sacar fotos de esos air roots. Big ol' long, dangling, and twisted raíces, starting, some of them, fifteen or twenty feet off the ground. Pocas veces he visto eso and never, que yo recuerde, in this country. En Puerto Rico, near that ritzy hotel en el Viejo San Juan y luego en Magnetic Island, en 2006 (both times con Pierre y el Paulie, fíjate). Off the Queensland coast, en Australia. Pero eso fue tropi-flora, en los mangroves, y esto a pleno oak and redwood forest. Strange. O quizás no. Más bien directamente emblemática del *ars combinatoria,* del shuttle-movement back and forth, in-between, que constituyen mis travels. Mis vivencias. Mi escritura. My life.

Varias veces estuve a punto de convencerme de que el cougar was lying in wait—sprawled or crouched, indolent or alert—en una rama arriba del sendero. Eran pasadas las 11 de la mañana, not its natural hunting hour, me dije. Still, confieso que me puse a cantar. Like before, esa incongruente canción, decades-old, de Silvio Rodríguez. You know, with the chorus "nadie se va a morir, menos ahora . . ." Eso—that staunch yet achingly lyrical, more-than-thirty-year-old revolutionary fervor— espantaría a cualquier modern predator, ¿qué no?

Bajé, salí disparada de ese primaeval bohque y me metí en el Asian-inflected, paved path, al lado del lawn. Suddenly, al lado izquierdo, vi un startlingly green bush. I'd never even noticed it before, pero it had apparently flowered desde la última vez que caminé por allí. El lunes pasado it must've been, porque tuve que suspender los health walks por el extreme heat, all last week. So, anygüey, muñeca, no me digas que you hate summer, *nê*? Look what it brings: like an underwater creature right out of *The Little Mermaid* (OJITO: versión original, no Disney), se me apareció, waving and shimmying its four-inch-long, suddenly budded shoots en la brisa. Some kind of impossible, moss-colored coral. Sharp looking y droopy a la vez, somehow. Nunca había visto tal cosa en la vida. It was . . . just green. I mean, no tenía perfume ni brightly colored flowers, pero estaba outrageously, baroquely green.

Aquí en el Montalvo estoy descubriendo all the different permutations and iterations of "just" green. Como todos los shades y textures de green que rodean en la selva al Mr. Abel, el narrador de *Green Mansions,* my favorite book from eighth grade.

Yesterday, as we drove through the twisty, giant-redwood-lined back roads en el leather-upholstered, sun-roofed, smooth girlvoice-GPS-outfitted, late-model white Acura de mi amiga la Mary Raz, aka la Cronopia, I wished for a cuaderno, for *any* paper. Para tomar apuntes sobre la flora y fauna, like I used to do in Argentina. La Mary es madre de mi hatched advisee, el Jon Raz, y fíjate que ella vive less than half a mile from Montalvo. Me escapo con ella casi todos los weekends, y nuestros road trips y adventures constituyen un perfecto RX cuando el ambiente retretesco se pone demasiado intenso, too hothouse-y. Le puse ese nickname por su maiden name, Cronopoulos, pero it fits her, perfectly. She *is* a cronopia, y creo que Cortázar would agree.

Anygüey, this is NoCal green. This was my home. Pero, ¿y ahora?

Después de este sudden burst of early summer green, a little farther along the path, del otro lado, observé semi-melancólica que el Australian bottlebrush estaba on its last legs. Bien scraggly, desplumada. En vano busqué al colibrí en sus ramas. Quería ver si se repetía last week's milagro: un colibrí posado. Do you know how rare that is? Pero nada. Pero, isn't that la definición *misma* de un miracle anyway, me pregunté medio sourly—¿que no se repite?

I did find, sin embargo, como engarzadas en las ramas muertas del bottlebrush, a cache of those little round, spiny, sea urchiny, hollow, stemmed pods. Se habían caído de un árbol vecino, and gotten lodged in the lower thicket of bottlebrush branches. Hot tears saltaron, instant and automatic, as I reached up for one. These pods were, quizás, Mom's most idiosyncratic (bizarre, perfect for a Scorpio) Christmas decoration: we'd collect them for her, in the Valley, y luego los hacía spray paint con esa laca. Silver and gold. Y luego los metía, todos los años, entre las ramas del Christmas tree. Siempre que los veo, they remind me of Mom. Digo, de mamá en su heyday. Antes de que muriera Daddy y que ella se quedara inválida, paralyzed, en su casa en Santa Cruz donde por fin murió, en el '03. After fourteen years de esa jodida parálisis. Un alivio. Ay, pero esa es otra.

Bueno, luego de ese intensely emo-laden interlude proseguí hacia el Formal Garden del Senator Phelan (Little Eye, eh: Supe recién que he was an anti-Semite *y* que tenía una amante Jewish. Typical, hey? Fixation and disavowal a la vez . . .). I went in, for a change, through the gate on the right. Quería fotografiar las paper flowers. Secretly (bueno, ni tanto), también me había sobrevenido una obsesión hacia el hummingbird. I suddenly remembered I'd seen another one last week, posado. Right here, en mi secreto recinto. Se había quedado absolutely still, mucho pero un chingo de tiempo, en la frondosísima rama de un silk tree. De hecho cuando hubo movimiento it was I, finally, who moved.

Me alejé only reluctantly, rubbing my neck, semi-stiff por haber estado craning, peering, tilted patrás embelesada por ese minúsculo still point.

I was certain it had been here, inside my secret garden, donde lo había visto. A mano izquierda, on the way to discovering the paper flowers. Pero no. Me equivoqué. Qué boluda—there aren't even any trees to speak of, before you come to the shocking stand—or grove, o como corno se le diga a grupo de flores—of paper flowers. Me tinca que son algún tipo de poppy (oh, I wish Mom could see them; she'd know for sure). Two, three, hasta five feet tall, crecen. Parece que se auto-propagan, en un sistema de runners. ¿No serán estos los famosos rhizomes, the ones D & G go on about? Oh my God, PoMo culti studies at the grass—o al menos—roots level. ¡Qué chévere! Pero anygüey, estas flores se desbordan; they spread right out into the little pebbled path, pushing their way más allá de la frontera del flowerbed, insistentes, desobedientes, audaces.

Me parecen un tipo de flor inexistente. Digo, directamente unreal. De fantasía. Los tallos son extremely long, flexibles, más bien pálidos. A dusty, almost sage green. Pero lo real(mente) maravilloso (*pace* Carpentier), astounding—aparte el perfume, pero I'll get there just now—son los pétalos. Son seis. Son enormes y blancos. Not optic white sino softer, creamy, bien opaque. Casi casi del color del Acura de la Cronopia Raz, pero sin ese sheen del Acura, casi opalescent. Los pétalos se ven crisp, crepe-papery. Pero they flop and sway, open and closed, en la brisa matutina. Versión miniatura y vegetal de oreja de elefante africano. Al centro tienen, te lo juro, una parte yellow-green, ferozmente erecta cual falo muñequeril, rodeado de un círculo perfecto de butter-yellow, pollen fuzzy-topped, teensy citron-colored antennae.

Y por si todo esto—the bold, fantasy look of them, quiero decir—no fuera suficientemente sublime, if you gather the papery petals together in your hand and sniff into the little cup, despiden un olor fresco, tenue, plasticky. Barely even plantlike. Barely even *there*. Un poco como el creosote, quizás (ese olor lo aprendí con el escritor 'tinísimo Eddie Muslip, en ese desert botanical garden, en Phoenix. Sé que suena a oxymoron, pero te juro, it *wasn't*. An oxymoron, quiero decir. Ese jardín was amazing, multicolor, and wildly perfumed). Pero pensándolo mejor, no. Not creosote after all. Nada pungent, or oily. El perfume no es verde, ni tampoco flowery. It's definitely culinary. Closest, al ponderarlo, al olor de la masa harina. On the other hand, it's *nothing* like the scent of the flowering plums que abundaban en Santa Cruz y me enloquecían mientras caminaba de vuelta a casa, de la Harbor High School. Estos mismos small, polite, purple-black leaved árboles que bordean el Thompson Creek trail en Claramonte (my at-home health walk). Cuando florecen—a brief, dizzying profusion of tiny, pale pink blossoms—allí por marzo, early April, siempre les he dicho los tortilla-flower trees.

I'll *never* quite get it, I reckon. I mean, con las palabras. Todo es aproximación. Y eso es lo más maddening—or magic—del olfato, ¿no?

Por su white, insouciant, papery look, por su semejanza a la amapola (scentless, a fin de cuentas, no obstante esa famosa escena de la Wicked Witch of the West, purring evilly, "Poppies, *poppies* will put them to sleep. Sleeeep, sleeep . . ."), when I leaned in to sniff, I hadn't been expecting any scent at all. Y por eso, el cool, familiar mounds of damp masa harina y Mercado Libertad en verano scent es—por lo utterly inesperado—lo más disturbingly, comfortingly, hechizante que tienen las paper flowers.

Stay with me a while. Busquemos, together, más strange familiars.

II

Montalvo Diary

Yo no puedo olvidar nada. Dicen que ese es mi problema.
Roberto Bolaño, *Amuleto*

¿Es de hierbabuena
o de azahares el olor?
¿Es de menta picante,
de cedrón o de tilo,
de margarita en flor
o de durazno?
No importa:
Algo del pasado despertó
Y nos ha emborrachado,
Nos ha puesto a soñar.
Cristina Piña, *Magia blanca*

The past isn't dead and buried. In fact, it isn't even past.
William Faulkner, *As I Lay Dying*

4-V-08
domingo

*M*e habré apendejado TANTO, en la vida cotidiana, I mean in my so-called (real) vida—todo predecible, safe, rutinario, protegida (by Pierre)—que ahora la más mínima desviación, cualquier ínfimo acto normal, "independiente" lo veo como GRAN hazaña and I'm soooo proud of myself, hasta me congratulo y me festejo y todo. Por ej: I just drove P. to the San José airport. It was like a dream. Como volver a pisar en, habitar un sueño recurrente. No me acuerdo if I'd ever actually driven there myself before, pero of course I'd been on this road so many times. Con mi papá, con mi familia. So todo era a la vez familiar y extraño. Ergo, la definición misma de lo *uncanny*.

La cosa es que hoy caminé—bueno, *hiked*—con Pierre por los trails aquí en Montalvo. It was spongy and green, pale, pebble-incrusted or pine-carpeted dirt. Me trajo todos los northern Califas feelings de antaño. Excepto lo del *puma*. *Yebo,* a fucking mountain lion was spotted, pero al ladito mero de esta mi miniatura, glass-walled tree house.

Me siento bien Robinson Crusoe. Pero repito: *why?* All I did was something people routinely do: drive someone to the airport. Get in a car and drive, in an unfamiliar part of the world (y ni siquiera es, del todo, unfamiliar). ¿Y qué? Y yo congratulándome, al volver sobre mis pasos: 880S to the 17S ("to Santa Cruz," I read the freeway signs medio wistfully), exit at Highway 9, go west un chingo (o tal parece), and turn in at the sign for the Montalvo Arboretum, en Saratoga. Pero, come *on*. I mean, look at el Paulie. Viene de Australia, alquila un "higher car," and drives (on the wrong side de la calle y todo) *all* over the show—dos meses.

Te acostumbrarás a estar sola de nuevo, I tell myself. Es sólo eso: cosa de acostumbrarse. These are *your* redwoods, *your* dweedly two- and three-lane highways. Thin lanes, in ill repair. Estos tus slower than L.A. pero el doble de erráticos NoCal drivers.

Smiling wryly to myself, I watch some dot-com hotdogger en un Lamborghini swoop up on my nalga en el retrovisor, zigzag past me, weaving in 'n' out cual murciélago del infierno. Because he *can,* me figuro. In L.A., todo tiene una grim precision en los freeways. It's so damn crowded, 24/7, one false move y eres tostada. Pero up here, the roads are curvier, bumpier, y simplemente hay menos autos on the road. Y estas condiciones explican la preponderancia de space cadettes y cowboys.

Estoy sola. Alone in this spartan, glass-walled studio, rodeada de verde y grillos. But I'm laughing. Pensando en ese vato en su orange-yellow, half-a-Lego Lamborghini. It's fucking *cold* at night here (se me había olvidado). I miss the "Girls," Esmeralda y Alejandra, mis hijas felinas, and P. Pero he estado sola antes. *Realmente* sola (think Africa, por ejemplo). Y sé que bregaré con esta soledad. No. Floreceré.

P.D. Speaking of flowering: Funny, en mi último sueño en casa, antes de salir para Montalvo, the April 26 one, I was inside a glass-walled structure (check). I was choosing bunches of tuberose (check). Ayer entré a una floristería pa' pedirle al dueño *brekkie* advice. In a bucket, right at the entrance, había NARDOS: fifteen dollars a bunch! Mi flor preferida, bar none. El vato me explicó que they were "the first of the season." Por eso tan caros. No los compré. Pero I'll go back, mos def.

6-V-08

Ayer fue un día increíble. I wrote the whole day. Alguna gente no entiende que lo que les mandé por e-mail *fue* una crónica. Capaz because it was only my second day here, difícil creer que I've hit the ground running. Pero it *was,* coño. Digo, una crónica CDM, as God commands. Algunos interlocutores do not distinguish entre mis cartas, digo, my "normal" e-mails, mis diary jottings (que luego mando, *as* letters) y una crónica. Or, piensan que todo es crónica. (What *is* the difference, anygüey?) Revelation (ja ja): Quizás sea, more than anything, la falta de distractions lo que hace un escritor. No one to talk to (los daily yarns I spin for P. . . .), no place to go. Except *inward.* Me sentí enérgica and yet, also, intensely focused. With a singular, odd intensity.

Todo fue extraño, slowed down yet also charged. No puedo creer que ese handyman Steve (Earle!) se haya quedado dos horas aquí! He has that sort of Califas born and bred (which he *is*), hipster, know-it-all tone. And the singular inability to detect, parece, when he's overstayed his welcome and you'd like nothing better than to get back to what you were doing. Es bien nice, sin embargo, y parece que he fixed la ducha y esperemos, la eccéntrica sliding door to the studio, arriba. Still, es medio tcjón.

¿Los otros artistas? So far (two days on!), el más impresionante parece ser un arquitecto. Tiene cierto parecido con Jason Patric, circa *The Lost Boys*. Tiene una especie de Ph.D. tripartito: de Sevilla, París y Roma. He doesn't seem, at first blush anyway (digo, after the communal dinner de anoche; no obstante, I think I semi-dread los dinners . . .), demasiado stuck up.

Hoy, ejercicio de la memoria. I wonder how I've avoided reading my old diary all these years? The one I kept in 1982, before I moved to South Africa para estar con Howard. For some reason, en los meses antes de venir a este Retrete me obsesioné con la idea de traerlo para acá. Leerlo. Volver a ese lugar, ese país, South Africa. Y quizás más importante, al *before*. To what impelled me to go there: Howard.

Hoy, I've lanced myself. Uf! Algunas partes algo over the top; era *tan* intransigente, tan earnest, so politicized, passionate. I cringe! At the "me" writing, then. Un poco el feeling de cuando estaba en Princeton last fall, staying con Santo-Amor, leyendo los (unexpurgated!) diarios de Alejandra Pizarnik. Sensación de extranjería y reconocimiento, a la vez. Un poco creepy, voyeuristic y también, de algún modo, like a homecoming.

It's like reading the diary of another person. And yet, not a stranger exactly. Es decir, me reconozco aquí en las páginas. Pero a la vez, la operación de leer—y con lápiz y todo—*eso* es lo que se parece a cuando estuve en los archives de la Princeton library, fishing through los Pizarnik diaries. Looking for signs of . . . ¿qué? The woman I would become, that I *have* become? ¿La escritora?

7-V-08

*D*espués de pasar siete horas ayer, reading my 1982 diary, estuve como aturdida. I could hardly pull myself back into el mundo para ir a comer. I felt dizzy, extra-planetaria. Pero I'm glad I went down to the commons after all—la gente me pareció bastante normal anoche, nicer.

Right after dinner, patrás en la montura. Subí arriba, up the spiral staircase, al tree house. Así le digo al writing loft. Estoy aprendiendo un chingo (about the world, about me) de ese antiguo diario. It's not embarrassing like I thought initially. Not really. Soy muy despiadada conmigo misma. I've *always* been like that. It's my Saturn in the twelfth house, supongo.

8-V-08

*E*n esta caja de cristal, el sol penetra a todo dar, 'mano. From about maybe 5 a.m. on. Bajé y comencé a leer el giraffe-print diary, el que me regalaron Mom and Daddy as a going-away gift, cuando me iba a Sudáfrica. It takes courage, encararme con eso. Tanto dolor allí dentro, Dios mío. A pesar de todo el amor, del deseo pasional, the way we were in my country, almost right from when I first pitched up in Jo'burg, a casa de la familia de H., me sentí lost, enraged, betrayed. No pude menos que echarle la culpa a él, or could I? Ah, it sounds ridiculous now—to the "me" now, reading this—to "blame" him, to hold him accountable for the evils of apartheid. Pero at the time, I felt like I was dying. No pude quedarme allí, en South Africa, y quedarme con él. I couldn't make it make sense. Decidí quedarme. Quedarme a vivir, pero vivir . . . en contra. Una decisión pírrica, in many ways. Could *never* call it a victory, just a way out. Very bloody. Oh, esta lectura me está rajando.

There's a hawk, wheeling and screeching, calling insistently. Mi emblema, mi totem. Salí afuera; my eyes scanned the ridge of eucalypti at the top of the hill, above los live-work studios. Pero no lo veo. Where are you? Who are you calling?

10-V-08

This Retrete is bringing back—with great immediacy and clarity—people from my past. Gente de San Francisco/Berkeley. Y de South Africa. Sobre todo de allí. Oh, Howard.

13-V-08

Ayer muy solitario. Caminé. Me obsesioné estúpidamente con la idea de que el mountain lion me acechaba! Me salí del sendero, just briefly (like el moteca de Cortázar!), and right there I felt doomed, scrabbling through the underbrush—leaves, roots. Todo horriblemente slippery. I could see the amphitheater, just below. Pero me convencí de que el tigre me veía también y que con un zarpazo me agarraba. Ridiculous, lo sé. Son criaturas solitarias, ariscas. Pero yo misma, LITTLE EYE: no del todo unlike them—arisca y a veces (aunque sólo a veces) solitaria *in extremis,* directamente huraña—I guess las imágenes de *Cat People* o bueno, even that Disney movie (¿cómo corno se llama?) are etched too firmly en mi subconsciente como para que la lógica tenga chance. Not while I'm en el bosque, anygüey . . .

Luego decidí intentar un *ars combinatoria*: una crónica sobre este (unfounded?) terror andante y otro. De hace unos veinticinco años. Fuck. When I was walking alone in Pretoria y fui abordada por un africano (digo, negro) who sidled up to me and asked me what I was afraid of. We walked along, side by side. Y hablamos. In my terrible guilt—at having gone to live in South Africa durante el apartheid, at being consistently privileged, (mis)taken as white (instead of coloured)—I clung to the idea, hope, illusion de que el vato no me habría abordado así, not in a million years, si me hubiera creído sudafricana. Silly, quizás. The common threads: walking (ahora una forest flaneur, entonces, de urbe) and el miedo.

What *am* I afraid of? ¿Por qué postergo tanto la verdadera, *auténtica* writing (en pro de mi diario, mi correspondencia, I mean), la escritura de "la cosa"? Pero, ¿qué *es* la cosa? Scholarly writing? Only? An academic tome (en estos tiempos de flatlining academic publishing)? Is *that* what a "real" book means to me? Still? ¿Por qué siempre algo . . . something else, something other, tan out of reach? Nunca satisfecha . . .

Recuerda. Burn this into your brain, mija: that hideous, disappointing scene in André Aciman's *Call Me by Your Name* (*such* an inspired regalo, de mi adorado Santo-Amor) cuando el narrador finds that *oke* he'd had the passionate, violently erotic affair with in Italy—a los diecisiete años. It's maybe only seven to ten years later, pero el otro vato es profesor. Casado. And . . . there's regret for our hero, pero no. It's something else. El reconocimiento de que that was *it*—or *could've* been it. Pero el otro se fugó, regresó a su vida. Cotidiana, normal. Se casó. He chose safety.

¿Y yo? Have *I* become insoportablemente aburrida myself, ¿o qué? Boring, because I've survived?

15-V-08
Ola de calor

Estoy leyendo una memoir, *When She Was White*. Y voy a (re)leer *David's Story* by Zoe Wicomb. Me hechiza. This novel—y cosas que yo misma escribí hace casi veintiséis años, en mi diario de 1982—han fomentado un deep e-mail exchange with Wim. I mean, renewed. Con renovado ahínco. Sobre la identidad dizque coloured ("colorados," we faux-translate, adrede, together. Fíjate que según Wimmie, muchos de los Chicanos, los U.S. Latinos, *look* like the coloured community he ministers to en la Ciudad del Cabo), por ejemplo. Mi obsesión.

16-V-08

Ayer, un horror. Calor. *Unbelievably* hot. En la tarde, te juro que it was actually hotter *inside* this glass-walled cube que afuera. Cero air circulation. Who the fuck was the imbécil, egger dizque arquitecto who designed this? Quién en su right mind idearía un west-facing, *all* glass wall, sin ventanas? Quisiera tener un BB gun para shoot out algunos de estos glass panels. Get some air. Ahhhh, no aguanto.

Cuanto más lo pienso, más importante es lo que me escribió la Joanna Woolfolk, mi astróloga, about this time at Montalvo being about becoming whole. Suena un poco touchy-feely, New Agey (and I'm *so* . . . not; ni la Joanna tampoco), pero it makes sense, al pensarlo.

Instead of remaining distanced from, afraid to face la que era hace veinticinco, veintiséis años. Not wanting to see, to remember, cómo proyecté todo en Howard. My own guilt, mi miedo. My reconnecting with Howard now. Duele, de algún modo. Un chingo. Makes me remember too much. Toda esa promesa, San Francisco– and New Orleans–born, and what we did, what *I* did to it. What South Africa did to us. Creo que este impulso es un modo de, un intento de . . . reconciliar (ja ja, my own *private* Truth and Reconciliation Commission, hey?). Un sentirme, sí, más íntegra. Instead of fragmented. O, digamos, parcial. Cut off (por el miedo de reconocer mi parte en nuestra separación) de ese momento tan wrenching, tan formative. My San Francisco and South Africa self. Escindida de mi pasado. De Howard. De la que fui. Y sigo siendo, coño. Because I *am* still her, ¿no? Ella es yo. (Uf, little Miss Raza-Rimbaud wannabe, ¿o qué?)

17-V-08

Revelación de hoy: It doesn't have to have lasted or "worked out" para ser amor.

19-V-08

Fantastic day. Went to San Francisco w/ la Cronopia Raz. Almorzamos en Greens, ese famoso, vegetarian-luxe restó in the Marina. En Fort Mason. Luego fuimos a North Beach a tomar café. We went into a little place on Columbus (OB-vio) and were waited on by two apparent Calabresi (por los afiches que había all over the walls). Uno se creía *bien* capo. Conversaban entre ellos en un dialecto (sounded vaguely Sicilian) y al salir (they'd been eying us all the while) les dije, "Ciao, grazie." This occasioned an avalancha of *sorrisi,* "ciao, bella," etc.

Luego, we drove through la City con la Cronopia en su smooth-as-seda, pearlescent white Acura, through Russian Hill, Pacific Heights, down through the Marina—*my* Marina—going east on Lombard, pasando el Marina Safeway. La Trish, mi roomate de antaño, and I used to call it Swingles-way, tan notorio era el lugar para hookups en los produce aisles; we used to walk all the way there, desde 2370 Chestnut Street, entre Scott y Divisadero. La Chestnut Street. Mi calle.

Hacía fresco (57 degrees!), a perfect summer day, según yo. Ya sé, ya sé. Ridiculously chilly for almost verano. Pero hey, es San Francisco. And anygüey, de que yo tenga Seasonal Affective Disorder al revés has already been established. Mucha neblina. I felt refreshed, relieved. Era estar, de nuevo, en todos esos mis lugares, places que me significaban Howard. O yo sola, intensamente viva. Después de estos tres o cuatro días de relentless, inescapable heat en Montalvo (me tenían flayed, splayed out, feeling sluggish, hibernational, swollen like a watermelon), it was invigorating, y bien reassuring, to feel the remembering kicked into high gear again, the fierce hunger to form words on the page returning. Esto es lo que quiero. This is what I live for. My heart (in S.F.) felt dark and pulpy, intensely beating, fragile, close to melting. Alive, alive.

La memoria *me derrite.*

21-V-08

La visita de mi hermana Sarita was chévere. Pero *bien* unsettling. Her recuerdos so often corroborate (or supplement) mine. Recordaba—me recordó—that I'd gotten pregnant w/ Howard, in 1982. Y que tuvimos un miscarriage. En el Mardi Gras, en New Orleans. Coño, si yo (with my legendary memoria de elefante) *no* me acordaba de eso. Until I confirmed it, en mi diario. En ese cuaderno chino de 1982. I had blocked that memory totally, suppressed it. Todos estos veintiséis años. When she told me, y después, cuando me obligué a leer a esas páginas, me pegó una ola de dolor, all the feelings of loss from twenty-six years ago—de tremenda promesa y amor, lost. I had to lie down and sob. Keening sobs, descontrolada. Unlike me. Bueno, I cry, OB-vio. A lot, even. Pero no tiendo a ser histérica. Kind of alarmante. *This* was what I'd been trying to keep myself (safe) from, then. Estos memories. *Este* ür-recuerdo en particular. Digo, al no abrir el diario, esa caja de Pandora.

22-V-08

*L*a memoria se somatiza. Esto es cierto. Tanto he estado, these last few weeks, *a la recherche de* . . . looking into me (OMG, sounds like una Jackson Browne song), into that anodynely beige-covered Chinese cuaderno from 1982, that the experiences and feelings recorded there se me están (in)filtrando. Isn't that a fairly conventional literary and filmic conceit anyway? Tener a la protagonista fishing through someone's diary or letters (someone historical or famous, usually) to the point that she starts to identify—to become, to *embody*—that other person en los textos? Well, esto es lo que me está pasando. Except the (other) person in the text *c'est moi*!

Ayer me obligué a leer las entradas de March 1982, about that miscarriage I'd had, con Howard. And then I wrote here, en *este* diario, about how my sister Sarita had brought it up, así no más—*she* remembered it, though I'd suppressed it completely. Bueno, anyway now—desde ayer—blood. Sólo *días* después de sentir, intensely, la ovulación. *Exactly* like what happened to me, to my body, then.

Why is it only *now,* precisely now, I come back to this 1982 diary? Si lo tuve allí, *right* there in my study, all these years? Ese diario, it's just like the ruby slippers: they were the fetish-object that conjured the result, always already (*pace* Derrida) available a la Dorothy, all along: volver a casa. Abrir ese cuaderno beige consituye, in some strange yet fundamental way, un homecoming for me.

Acabo de re-leer la entrada en mi diario actual, the last entry before I came to Montalvo, sobre aquel sueño del 26 de abril. Cada vez que lo leo me parece más prophetic. No sólo la parte de la glass-walled structure in the dream (and I'm living in one *now,* literalmente) y los nardos, sino también lo del earthquake. Quizás especially that part. Porque el temblor is happening *now,* inside me. El recuerdo de esa pérdida. So brief, pero so yearned for, somehow—that little zygote—aunque suene unbelievable ahora. Y luego tanta sangre, Dios mío. So much blood. How could I possibly block that out for so many years?

Recibí un e-mail de Howard. He *remembers.* Me escribió algo así como que hay un welter of thoughts/feelings rolling around inside him, all good. Orale. Mi escritura hace eso.

23-V-08

*E*s temprano. OMG: hay un overpowering olor a humo—I feared a fire was literally just over the ridge, through the trees—¡que tuviera que evacuar! What the hell would I grab? Mos def my computer. Los diarios. OB-vio, mis perfumes! Mi hermana Sarita just called. Me dijo que there was—IS—a HUGE incendio, started yesterday, en Santa Cruz! It was on CNN, como también shocking noticias of xenophobic violencia against immigrants in South Africa! ¿Qué está pasando? Part of my past burning up. Burning away. Esos extraños, harsh winds de ayer, they must've fanned it. Hoy quiero—necesito—escribir.

Es tan powerful, tan overwhelming, to read that diary. To *allow* myself to do that. To compel myself to do it: to go back and feel. Suena medio hokey, ya lo sé, pero te juro que as I read, estoy *allí* de nuevo. I meet up with . . . myself, encounter parts of me I'd sealed off. Pero not cauterized altogether, OB-vio. The pain of desire is there, esa haunting presencia de una ausencia, *pace* Lacan: raw, it can be retrieved, revived too, en esta relectura, in my broad, calligraphic fuchsia pen-strokes en la página. Coupled, now, with a keening pain, the awareness, no, el *reconocimiento,* de la pérdida. How *could* that force, so alive—have been sundered? And yet it was. I did. Howard and I did.

Terminé de leer y subrayar el diario. Hoy, a las 11:13 a.m. Hay un olor acre. A humo. Tengo las manos y los pies entumecidos. Pero I'm glad. Lo celebro. El diario termina el 29-VI-82. Yo, horrorizada por la probabilidad de no encontrar work en RSA, in the Republic of South Africa.

Terrified. Pero la última imagen es significativa: I assert myelf, mi "destino," as a writer. Uf, took you *long* enough to get there, muñeca!

24-V-08

H. me escribió otro e-mail. Laconic capricornio's gone almost prolific! Me dijo que he remembered, "clearly," el miscarriage. Según, recordaba eso "and a lot of other things."

Ah, alivio. The pain, el remordimiento, is *not* just yours. Not then, and—even after all this time—not now. A verrrrr. Tendré que re-ajustar todos mis paradigmas memorialísticos (uf! *What* a 'Tine you are, *alla fine*).

Escribí *todo* el día. I worked on that diary cual si fuera el documento de otro. Underlining, marking pages, and then typing it into the computer. Se lo voy a mandar a Howard. Me ha sobrevenido una sensación de urgencia: I need to know that he remembers *everything*. I need to remind him.

En 1982 Howard y yo llamábamos "el Transcript" a ese running diario/chronicle I used to keep. I carried it with me everywhere: en el BART over to my T.A. job en Berkeley, en nuestro road trip al Mardi Gras. Cuando H. regresó a Sudáfrica, yo copiaba las entries, by hand, y se lo mandaba a él en Jo'burg, como cartas. Well, they *were* letters, ¿no? En fin: I wanted to end today on a high note, este día extraño, exaltado, tan through the looking glass.

25-V-08

*W*ho am I? ¿Qué busco? ¿Por qué este journey into my past, ahora? Y si lo que busco es confirmación de la "realidad" de la relación, de mi impacto en H., de su amor, well, has he not *given* it to me, varias veces y readily (even in his own parco, Goat-Boy way), just recently? So, ¿qué *más* busco? Ah, mija: you're *such* a connection junkie.

LITTLE EYE: Wimmie thinks it's crucial que todo esto me esté ocurriendo ahora, precisely now, right at this juncture when northern Califas is burning and South Africa is burning, burning in the townships again, *just* like when I lived there.

Me siento abandoned, solitary. Insular. Es difícil. Sola, sola. Tres semanas. And yet: after all this radical soledad, ¿cómo me sentiré on reintegrating myself w/ human company? Completely alone el viernes, and yesterday. All day. And yet I wanted it, *craved* it, even, to commune with my memories y la escritura and the disturbing, moving thoughts and feelings they stir in me. Y en los otros.

29-V-08

*H*as all this—todo este memory-trove—been here all along, digo, dentro de mí, y yo simplemente unaware? Just like el *click click click* de los ruby slippers, coño. Y estoy patrás; it's so intensely present, como si estuviera conviviendo, again, con los strange familiars, all the principals de esa época. Pero the main focus of this memory vortex is mos def Howard. This is all about my Berkeley and Marina days, mis San Francisco days (gracias, Chris Isaak). And I am conjuring them—los recuerdos, los personajes mismos—with my dreams, with my writing.

Subí para checar mi horóscopo on the computer. Los astros were auspicious: for writing, for my reading tonight en el Barnes & Noble en el Pruneyard, en Campbell. Also for remembering, for surrounding myself w/ the familiar made uncanny—unheimlich (amo esta palabra)— by its startling return to me, después de años, *décadas* missing (missing, pero *not* perdido, as Wim reminded me).

1-VI-08

*P*ierre me vino a visitar y repasamos ayer los greatest hits, los replays (posibles, or at least factibles), de mi San Francisco. ¿Habré cambiado yo tanto que ya no puedo regresar, no longer recognize myself en estos landscapes urbanos? Aquí en S.F., donde antaño I walked—confident or lonely pero mos def flaneur (EYE: OB-vio, I *know* this is the masculine version de la palabra, pero ever since reading ese ensayo de la Debbie Castle, en su libro *Easy Women,* no way can I write *flaneuse,* pos según la Debbie, eso equivale a streetwalker): dueña, anygüey, de estas S.F. streets. Ay, chill out, muñeca. *Such* a drama queen. Change happens. Y . . . aceptalo, ¿queréh?

2-VI-08

*P*ierre here and gone, todo demasiado rápido. Pero S.F. was be-YOND. It was cold (mid-50s!), overcast (para variar). We took the 280N desde el Retrete and then Highway 1, entrando por el Parque Golden Gate, just like we used to. Through the Sunset, the foggy Richmond. Thru the Presidio and down to the Marina. And oh, aunque la Marina ahora esté past its prime, just a herpes-triangle after all, como quien dice, for burly, gringo, rich frat boys (coño, was it *always* like that, y no me daba cuenta? Quizás un little hair . . . pero había algo . . . something different too, wilder. Or was that just us?), *siempre* amaré la Marina. Cow Hollow. Bueno, chale to Cow Hollow, and for sure not Union Street. Eso *siempre* fue yuppie central. But Chestnut Street—mi calle—with its funky eateries, oldtime Italian delis, like Lucca Delicatessen, a block and a half al este de nuestro apartamento. And walking walking walking, con mi roommate la Trish, the two blocks east and a few over, up Fillmore, todos los jueves, to the corner of Greenwich and Fillmore, ese nuestro zenith: the Balboa Café.

For some reason todo habrá comenzado aquí, ¿no? "The Boys"—Howard y sus amigos, Ken y el Du Toit—los tres sudafricanos on international, post-university holiday, could so easily have gone to L.A., a otro bar. De hecho, they *had* started the night en otro bar, en Rosebud's on Union Square (uf, *long* gone). Dizque English pub on the ground floor del hotel St. Francis, donde habían conocido a mis amigas, Helen and Tina. Ellas y otra amiga, la Pamela, trabajaban de saucy-wench cocktail waitresses. Te lo juro: dirndl skirts, corsets, blusas bien escotadas con mutton-chop mangas. Ay, suena bien cheesy ahora, pero what can I say? It was the '80s. Yo iba un chingo a Rosebud's during my last few months in S.F., my Penelope-espera, waiting to be reunited w/ Howard. Iba a tomar double Rémys, waiting for Helen or Tina or Pamela to get off work.

Pero why *then,* esa noche en particular, el 28 de enero del '82, if not precisely and *only* para que H. y yo nos conociéramos? He walked by esos huge plate-glass windows del Balboa Café, vitrineando como dijera Lemebel, our eyes met . . . and the rest was—*es*—(t)history.

Yo sigo, empedernidamente believing in fate. El destino. El sino. El hado. Aunque esté fuera de moda. Y aunque las cosas no siempre salgan happily ever after . . .

5-VI-08

*U*n mes, llevo aquí in my own private green mansions. Conocí a mi vecino el martes. Vi que la residency manageress, la Julie, merodeaba con un unknown vato outside el estudio next door to me. So, después de un mes de absoluta, prístina soledad, el Troll Grotto next door estará ocupado. How do I feel about that? Levemente como . . . invadida. Irritada, even. Veremos.

El tipo mandaba vibes medio interesantes, so les seguí down the hill, por el parking lot. Vi que subían por el creek trail, los dos, con el Toto o cómo se llama. That little Toto-esque dog de la Julie. Oh yeah, Griffin. For some unknown, perverse razón, I kept following them, through the dense underbrush (ja, *that* would be good, suena al comienzo de un fairy tale bien thrilling. Pero debo confesar que hay un sendero through these woods, a paved one even, si bien está muy slick y al menos slightly peligroso por la cantidad de pine needles and eucalyptus pods underfoot, y el poison oak, pero a borbotones, a ambos lados del trail).

Luego gente, I swear I don't know what came over me, pero I growled at them. Simón, me salieron a couple of *real* good gruñidos. Howard me había enseñado a imitar los animal sounds del African bush (hasta me mandó un cassette, recuerdo, so I could perfect my imitaciones)—tipo, you know, león, wildebeest, hippo, hyena, baboon—y bueno, I've always been pretty crackshot con mis imitaciones, no importa la especie (esa habilidad la heredé de mi papá). So, desde que estoy aquí en el Montalvo, I've been working on my mountain lion. Bueno, first I did a couple of kind of low, chuffing ones. Nada. I *was* pretty far behind them, so, solté some slightly louder, more menacing ones. El Toto skittled about, bien nerviosito. Y el vato *did* kind of look around, too.

At trail's end, up at the top, cerca del lawn de la villa, I caught up to them. Thank God, no me asociaron—al parecer—con los menacing forest sounds. I just kind of stood there, bien geeky, in my ancient, black stretch health pants de Target, my tissue-weight yoga shirt, y mis on-purpose desesquilibrantes Chung Shi shoes. La Julie se apresuró para presentarnos y me invitó a acompañarles. She was giving the newcomer a tour. Bueno, anyway, ese era el Adán, my new next-door neighbor. Un Chicano film studies Ph.D. student, y también aspiring filmmaker and visual artist. Fue con él y la Julie que pude penetrar por primera vez a la villa. I'm sure I could've gotten inside there before, pero como que . . . nunca se me había antojado.

Lo mejor de ayer: two incredible hawk sightings. Uno arriba, just this side of the ridge, de ese stand de eucalyptus where I often hear them. El Adán se apuntó para acompañarme, on my health walk. Not sure how I feel about going *with* someone. Será una experiencia . . . *otra,* that's for sure. He estado *tan* y tan sola. Am I ready to return to human company? O ¿sería mejor que continúe, como personaje de Pizarnik, como alguien que no ha dejado de morar en el bosque? Me siento conflicted.

The first hawk was circling real low. Buscando presa. El Adán le sacó un chingo de fotos. His camera is so teensy, pensé que era su teléfono, pero no. It's a real camera, como Dios manda. Ese halcón finally settled on a branch, way high up en un árbol. Luego vimos otro, when we were sitting on the bench detrás del Templo del (no) Amor.

6-VI-08

Me siento invadida, mos def. Don't get me wrong (como dice mi máxima carnala en Claramonte, Deborah Barker-Benfield, "la B-2"): el

Adán es cool. Pero I'd feel this way no matter con quien. Could be him, could be anybody. Es que este Retrete, up to now, had been *so* much about solitude, una productividad bien prodigious, concentrada. Había perdido totalmente la costumbre, la paciencia para normal social interaction. La intensidad de un aloneness I hadn't experienced en años. Me había acostumbrado, was even savoring it. Tendrá que ver con mi Mercury en la casa tres, en Piscis. Reconozco ser hipersensible (uf, qué pesada).

Me quedé todo el día en la torre (¡el Adán le dice "el castillo de la pureza"!), writing. The dinner was awful. Lo que se dice *awful*. El arquitecto ya ni se digna a bajar a los commons anymore, so it wasn't that. Digo *him*, su soberbia, faux-intense, tejoneante presencia. El vato se aísla ahora completely con la egger de su French novia. Pero el Retrete es, ahora, puros vatos and me, basically. They're a bunch of techno-geeks, te lo juro. Está un tal Lutero y su sidekick el Carlo, un Ph.D. student cubano que no habla español. Digo, he understands, y creo que *podría* hablar if he wanted to. Pero he never does. Siempre contesta patrás in English. Anda siempre leather jacketed, no matter what the weather, siempre vestido de puro *noir*.

Anyway, en el dinner platicaban de su truchísimo dizque avant-garde biometrics proyecto. No entiendo exactly qué coño *es* el proyecto, pero it seems they want to set up some machine, como para medir los brain waves de la gente (sounds bien retro, ¿no? Como *bien* Scientology). Decían que quieren instalar la tal machine over in Santana Row, ese yuppie mall (just like el Grove en L.A., pero filled to the brim con wealthy Middle Eastern and Asian shoppers). Yo me le reí en la cara al Lutero; le dije: You think Santana Row is "middle America"? Pero el vato, bien lelito, pobre, just looked at me, kinda smiling su Tom Petty–ish toothy grin, con el perfecto blank blue stare de un slightly largo en el diente antaño surfer boy, raised in Malibu (which he actually *was*).

Por suerte, I'd paid attention to my horóhcopo, which had warned me against any outbursts. Luego, comenzaron a hablar de karaoke, concepto que detesto. Finally, Jessie, la chef, me invitó a acompañarlos. I declined, horrorizada (OB-vio). Me fugué. Back up the hill al studio.

Me siento assailed on all sides. Dinner time, which was, en mayo, a relaxing, convivial highlight del día, se ha convertido en un miasma de testosterone. Joder. Todo esto viene a confirmar my fundamental discomfort with (most) hetero males. Si no hubiera encontrado a P. (o vice versa), I'm sure I'd have been with a woman. O sola.

Fui en el health walk. Sola. Allí en mi secret garden, detrás del boludesco Templo del (no) Amor—a former fountain composed of four hideously grinning satyrs with only the memory of a terremoto-toppled Venus at the center—the thought occurred to me que ahora soy yo la que dirijo mi propio sendero. O camino. Sounds like a *really* obvious, second-wave feministic proclamation, ¿qué no? Pero, ¿sabes qué? It's true.

Antaño me consideraba so free. Pero wasn't I always sort of . . . waiting for "something" to happen to me, in a way (léase: someone)? Oh, I made a good show of doing my own thing. Y en la superficie, se veía hasta pretty impressive. Estudié. I was good at it. I got into Harvard y todo. Pero look a little closer: me dropeé de la UC–Irvine para volver a Santa Cruz. To live with Nick, el escultor sureño, Vietnam vet. To be his muse (on food stamps). Y luego, bueno, I kept studying, sure. Pero bastante half-assedly. Kind of biding my time, sin rumbo (*pace* Cambaceres!), en Berkeley, San Francisco. Until being with Howard, going to South Africa, se convirtió en mi destino (hay que reconocer, to be fair: the academic job market *was* flatlining, bigtime, en los early '80s). No era sino hasta tomar la chamba en Pomona that I can say I was actually, completely directing myself. Mistress of my own path. Irónico. After all my world travels, todas mis mudanzas. Cuando agarré el puesto convencional, full time, con retirement y HMO y todo, *allí* es cuando comencé a sentirme realmente independent. Y por eso, en algún sentido, free.

¿Y ahora? It's my writing. Esto me dirige. Would I pull up and move, wait for someone, follow someone? No. No güey.

By the way: el árbol que está right below the poet's stairs, allí arriba, up by the Villa Montalvo? Es TILO. Just like the trees right underneath my bedroom window en Buenos Aires.

7-VI-08

*A*yer FATAL. Pobrecita. Me sentí edgy, lonely, lacking—todo el día. Nadie me está escribiendo lately, ¡coño! Not Howard, ni Wim tampoco. Raphy, el Santo-Amor, el Paulie, y Hugo ni hablar: *todos* los Musos, gone silent at once. And that is *so* much my juice. De donde derivo mi ímpetu. Para escribir. Para vivir. From faraway people. Their words. De esas ausencias presentes. De (im)posibilidades.

8-VI-08

*I'*m convinced I've found the space/place/time to say things, about myself in/and el mundo *in direct proportion* to having stopped the media madness. No digo que quiera continuar este ayuno permanentemente— against world events, por ejemplo (oh, Suid-Afrika!). Pero el newspaper. All my magazines, oh my God. Todos los jodidos work e-mails. How much I haven't missed them. En absoluto.

And this space inside me has opened me up to myself and also, paradójicamente (o ¿no?) al mundo.

On Going Back Crónica

1 June 2008
Saratoga, CA

For Carol Dell'Amico, Tina Schiller, and Pamela Williams,
and
for Yves Saint Laurent, in memoriam

I totally hear you, Caroltjie, in re: ¿cómo aguanto tanta nostalgia? How can I even bear up bajo el peso de volver (volver, volveRRRRR) este spring/incipiente verano, tanto revisiting de nuestros former lugares en el mundo: San Francisco, the Bay Area? Sudden, intense, este reliving, después de dos décadas away. Hubo muchos return visits, *natuurlik*. Pero that's *all* they were: two- to three-day escapadas de SoCal, cuando todavía hangueaba con los last remaining friends (so many had died of AIDS, or moved away . . .) como la Pamela W. misma, who held out in S.F. y luego Marin County, before decamping, finalmente, a Albuquerque este mismo año (OJO: she regrets this move, *bigtime,* se me hace).

Pero now, living en el Vortex (así le decimos al Retrete—aka el Montalvo Arts Center—my fellow artista y vecino Adán Avalos and I, por eso de que ni bien do you pass through its griffin-guarded gates, y se te chupa, como por alien attack, la cel reception), pos la City is *so* temptingly close que he ido un chingo de veces. Mostly con la Cronopia Raz, y esta vez, with Pierre.

I agree, it *is* pretty much kind of an exercise in torture, going back. No tanto en términos de encararme con (or admitting?) how much *I've* changed desde entonces. My deep Muso Wim, actualmente un Catholic priest que vive y trabaja en una coloured community en South Africa (whom I *really* want you to meet when he comes to visit este verano, Carol, por eso de tus cinco añitos en Port Elizabeth as a child; OB-vio, he was *far* from a priest, or even católico, for that matter, cuando lo conocí en Pretoria, he was raised Afrikaans, pero esa es otra . . .), dice que soy—sigo siendo, todavía, in so many ways—la misma mujer que escribió ese diary, you know, the one from 1982 (in which you feature prominently!) cuando vivía en S.F., in the Marina, on Chestnut Street, and I was trying to wrap my head around la decisión que ya había tomado mi corazón: mudarme a Sudáfrica para estar con Howard. Anyway, I've been rereading it, por primera vez in all these years—I'd never dared to before—en estas semanas en el Montalvo. Ponderando. Plundering. En casa, antes de salir para la residency, I'd resolved to crack that diario open there. Let it, quizás, hopefully, crack *me* open. Pero anygüey, como te decía, lo difícil para mí is more about . . . how much San Francisco has changed. En estas two and a half decades, post-SIDA, y luego, todo lo del dot-com boom y bust. *Tanta* yuppification y millonarios, all over the show. En Berkeley y Oakland también. Y el Castro. Tan hollow, somehow. Tan . . . *después*. Yuck. Casi irreconocible. What remains?

Pero you know what, Pierre y yo pasamos un mostly magnificent day here yesterday. Let's just call it un día de ethical flanerie (en tu honor). Yo diseñé la ruta (ya sabes: me fascinan los mapas). Estuvimos en la Marina, Pacific Heights, Fillmore Street, Union Square, North Beach. My old haunts. Por suerte, I didn't become *quite* as maudlin as I'm capable of (ja ja), pero sí tuve un momento algo grotesco en Union Square, donde antes salía del BART en la New Montgomery, al volver de dar mis clases en Berkeley. Remember? Al subir, to catch la 30-Stockton, pasaba muchas veces por Macy's. I would wander through the then (to me) *impossibly* elegant cosmetics floor. I browsed wistfully all over, pero me detenía más seguido en Christian Dior, para comprar un solitario nail lacquer, in "Cashmere," por ejemplo. (*This* was the epitome of lujo entonces, en un sueldito de miseria, as a grad. student!) O un blush, en "Fig." Or, si me sentía más flush, a bottle of my adored *Diorella*. El vibe era serene, sophisticated, relaxing. Reverential, o casi.

Bueno, ahora, it's all loud música enlatada, hot, over-bright halogen lights glinting off crowded, smudged mostradores. Not a saleslady in sight. Fragancias baratas, genéricas. Hordes of safe, anodyne "fruity-florals" como los de la J-Lo, o Paris Hilton o Jessica Simpson. O peor, casi, ese wishy-washy watery shit, que huele a faux-cucumber, como por ejemplo *l'Eau d'Issey* o *Acqua di Gio*. Gag. The whole floor desprovisto de cualquier glamour o misterio. Catering totally to MAC-ed out, apenitas post-teens. Le pregunté a Pierre: Estoy loca, or has this scene *completely* lost its élan? Aunque él no es, not by a long shot, un perfu-maniac como yo, estuvo de acuerdo: in general, los department store perfume counters se han vuelto total e irremediablemente inelegantes. Chatos. BOOORING.

Finally, I recovered a *semblance* de lo que había sido, years ago, la experiencia Macy's. En Saks Fifth Avenue. No recuerdo que este bastion of elegance and edginess—Saks is, after all, donde mi hermana la Wiggue, que *siempre* está en el último grito de la moda, trabajaba, up to last year, se me hace, de advertising copywriter—estuviera antes on Union Square. Pero I can't say for sure, porque creo que I would've been too cowed by my graduate-student-induced pobreza to even poner pie in there entonces.

Allí entramos, anygüey, looking for Thierry Mugler's new *A Travers le Miroir,* que yo había leído era un unusual tuberose scent. Como saben, enloquehco con el olor a nardo. Pero I mean *real* nardos, como los que venden en el Mercado de Abastos en Oaxaca. (Porque muchos de los perfumes que le dicen white florals, that feature tuberose, son si no directamente repugnantes, pues way too over-la-cima: *Poison* y *Fracas,* por ejemplo, or *Amarige*.) Es como dice ese personaje de Silvina Ocampo, en un short story. Algo así como: Los nardos me encantan, pero me descomponen. Yeah, creo que those are her exact words. Siempre quedé fascinada con eso de "la descomponen." Porque it's like that, *exactly* (pero in a good way, OB-vio): el olor a nardo *undoes* me.

Recuerdo hace dos o tres años, when I was teaching that story. Los estudiantes no tenían idea; quedaron completely perplexed. Les era insondable, ese oxímoron. So, traje oil of tuberose (synthetic, por supuesto, pero a pretty fair rendition, del Body Time, the one on Telegraph Avenue en Berkeley) y les unté . . . los essays (don't worry, Caroltjie! Como sabes, siendo también docente, *long* gone are the days where one could even dream of applying perfume a los pulse points estudiantiles! They'd throw our nalgas en la cárcel!).

Anyway, Pierre y yo must've looked like serious shoppers porque ni bien entramos we were seized and doted upon por un tipo que parecía Franco-Israeli, tipo el Chief, aka el Jack Abecassis, mi amigo, y antaño chair of my department (y antaño before *that*, back in la grad. school, beau—pero esa es otra). Ese fake-Chief passed us on to an owl-eyed, trucha-nailed (acrylics, thick and spatulate, ugh!) bottle blonde. La experta en Thierry Mugler, it seemed. Nos sacó cinco (!) perfumes en la serie "Through the Looking Glass," y dos se distinguieron: the tuberose one, que parecía promising (al menos, en el cardboard little swizzle stick) y otro, rarito, como de hierbas y vetiver (which I enJOY avidly).

I sprayed the nardo one en el antebrazo y merodeamos, algo sin rumbo (*pace* Cambaceres) por ese primer piso, semi-cowed por todos los extreme luxury goods (Prada bags, exotic and fascinating cosmetic lines, designer gafas de sol up the wazoo, etc.)—y eso que we didn't even make it up the escalator, a las designer *colleksies*! Porque unfortunately, después de sólo un ratito comenzó el drydown, and it wasn't pretty. Hasta comencé a detectar el dreaded "efecto Desenex." Así le bauticé al fenómeno que ocurre con algunos notorious scents that begin sexy and mysterious and almost liturgical, como el *Gucci Pour Homme*. Pero que luego, bueno . . . eso. They morph to athlete's foot powder.

OJO: That particular scent resulta que it smells divine en *todos* los Musos (bueno, except Hugo, and he could probably go for it too, tendremos que probar). Wim and I, hace dos años, went to el Nordstrom in Montclair Plaza (rasquache central, ese mall, but at *least* there's a Nordstrom), y allí tratamos de describir lo que buscamos a Teresa, my perfume lady there: something that combines the frankincense-y sublime de una iglesia católica con la scuzzy raunchiness of a (gently used!) men's locker room. Absolutely unruffled (pues me conoce hace años), la Teresa came up with *Gucci Pour Homme*. One whiff, one spritz and Wim agreed. Enthusiastically. Se lo regalé, y le fascina, bigtime. Pero he can *barely* give Mass in it, especialmente durante el verano en South Africa, pues it's *terribly* prone to inducing swooning, en masse, entre los feligreses. Can you imagine?

Al inspeccionar los botiquines en el baño de los Musos— respectivamente, Paulie Allatson (Sydney), Raphy Kadushin (Madison, WI), and Paul Saint-Amour (Princeton)—what did I verify? *Yebo: todos* los medicine cabinets lucían ese squat, golden elixir–filled cube! No coincidencia, OB-vio. Pero, psychicness museril no obstante, on *me,* el inicial soaring mystical note, followed closely by un utterly '80s-throwback raunch, casi de inmediato cede a un Desenex drydown.

So, reluctantly, Pierre y yo regresamos con la tecolote-eyed saleslady y le dije no, *A Travers le Miroir* doesn't transport me. It doesn't work on me. Se puso just a teensy bit grouchy. Bueno, *bahtante* huffy y casi casi a la defensiva, la verdad. (Um, no había muchos shoppers; are we in a recession yet, ¿o qué? Sure as hell *looks* like it.) Well, it *will* warm up on the skin, me dijo. This isn't "warm," le repliqué; it's athlete's foot powder! Entonces, como nos sentimos, immediately, pretty bad por ese outburst (la pobre, *so* close to scoring a big ol' commission . . . el Thierry ain't cheap!), Pierre me compró el 300 ml. bottle de *Eau de Ciel* de Annick Goutal. Are you familiar? Es una fragancia sublime: light pero todavía misteriosa. Mi hermana la Wiggue had given me her bottle, hace años in N.Y.C. Fíjate que I'd never replaced it when I used it up; *always* wanted to, pero nunca lo había encontrado, excepto en el Internido y siempre me daba flojera, so I sort of just went along, voluptuously coveting el recuerdo olfativo. Anygüey, it's *totally* appropriate for spring-summer, a base de hojas de violeta y rosewood.

Bueno, *natuurlik,* heme aquí gente, *already* fantasizing about my next conquista (typical MO of a true perfume junkie, ¿qué no?): I simply *must* sample *Carnal Flower* de Louis Malle, oops que digamos, el Frédéric Malle. También es a base de nardo, and helluva expensive. Supposedly the "truest" tuberose scent disponible en el mundo. Según, sólo se vende en Barneys New York.

Pero Pierre y yo no tuvimos tiempo siquiera de buscar el Barneys en Union Square, as we were off to our next assignation. Cenamos en Albona's, on Francisco Street, en North Beach. Results that es un unusual restaurant de Istria, recomendado por la Cronopia Raz. And no, Carol, not Ischia. Ya sé que es weird. Pero así de idiosincráticas y chéveres son, always, las recomendaciones de la Cronopia (hence el apodo). Istria ni siquiera es, en realidad, properly part of Italy hoy en día. Creo que es parte de Yugoslavia. Or maybe la *former* Yugoslavia? Pero ni modo: *that's* another story.

IV

San Francisco Transcript/ Diary

Distance is a proposition that points to an audience besides yourself.
Distance is a book.

Irene Vilar, *The Ladies' Gallery: A Memoir of Family Secrets*

Funny how things get away from you.
For years you can't remember nothing.
Then just like that, it all comes back to you.

Toni Morrison, *Song of Solomon*

Llevamos tanta sangre en los recuerdos
que a veces uno se siente culpable de ponerles límites,
de manearlos para que no nos inunden del todo.

Julio Cortázar, "Recortes de prensa"

24-V-08

Querido H.,

Here are some entries from my 1982 diary. I copied the entries—all of them, *longhand, nogal*!—and sent them to you as letters back then, remember? I've been looking at our Transcript again, here at this artists' retreat. Opening that little beige notebook has been like Pandora's box, the ruby slippers, and Aladdin's cueva all rolled into one: some *baie* powerful memory *muti,* in other words. It constitutes a kind of proof, somehow. And though I reckon you don't need proof (you *do* remember—"everything"—you e-mailed me yesterday), I'm sending you a few *seleksies* here anyway. My comments from now, today, in brackets, OK? Can you still hear my voice in these words? It is I, here, now, again, writing you again, asking you (for a change, hey?) to read, to feel, to remember.

9 - II - 82

*O*h, Howard. "Yes, my babe," you answered softly when I spoke your name. We slept not at all. And I *know* the last night, our last night [but it *wasn't*: you returned, dragging your friends Ken Steenkamp and Steve Du Toit with; you turned back from Tahoe, from the eastward drive, back toward a tidal lure] especially won't leave you, Montenegro [funny coincidence, or not: I have a colleague with the surname Montenegro, but for me, it is always—only—the name I called you after we saw Dušan Makavejev's film *Montenegro,* at the Bridge, out on Geary, remember? Your dark eyes and hair, the easy way you imitated the hero's sexy Central European cadences, his broken English. That was our script, we fantasized: being together in some exotic place, making love anywhere, everywhere; escaping banal, cold reality, igniting the screen of our lives in a burst of combustible passion]. I don't *care* where you are right now, honey. *Non ti scordar.*

15 - II - 82

*R*emembering now "The Last Night," as I call it. Tapes going. Need to record your voice, for later. You and I discussing apartheid heavily, with a thirst for each other's comments even at that late, late hour, Montenegro, mi amor.

Rain pouring down now. The telephone has never been so deadly silent, I've never in fact perceived its material composition in such minute detail; a somber, black, quiet object, churlish in its mute recalcitrance.

Alone with you, finally. For a moment, willing desire to come up through the wall of tears forming at the back of my throat and here, again, as I remember your mouth, your look as you nestled between my legs and took my thighs into your hands.

17-II-82

So much anticipation. I am ovulating furiously, and oh, damn, *right* on the eve of my "anniversary" reunion. Four Thursdays, exactly, since we met.

22-II-82

On the road. First time I feel *really* on the road, in that Kerouac way, the way I've always dreamed it. Semis passing by, warm Louisiana breeze blowing in, a straight ribbon of highway under the Dodge van wheels. Oh, but this dull pain is frightening. Ovulation slated for *last* Tuesday—a week ago. Felt a twinge, but really then . . . nothing. Then more definite, yes, an absolute thudding started Wednesday afternoon, just before the plane.

Here we are again. Together. Houston flat, concrete, large freeways. Drive out past dirt roads, coffee shops, gas stations. Pickups and cow-boy hats. Suburbia, sprawling ranch-style houses. I read the "Tran-script" to you in bed. Sharp pain continues on the left. I know what this means, but we make love anyway. Fast and furious, twice, before the lady of the house comes home!

24-II-82

So much to say because of left *unsaid* for days. Oh, the blood and the wonderment it caused. Fear. Pain. Togetherness. Cramps still here, pinching insistently. The blood is lessened, somewhat.

27-II-82

Mardi Gras. Remember Mardi Gras, Howard. Never forget. As we strolled down lower Bourbon Street during the daytime Sunday, quite near the house we said we wanted [1315 Bourbon Street—I've passed it *many* times since, always think of you], a dapper, middle-aged Southern homeowner took a quick look at me in your fedora and safari clothes, then did a kind of double take at us, together, and called out to you from his doorway, "To your *health,* sir!" You smiled and acknowledged, and lovingly bent down to put a slip of paper between leather thongs and my abraded ankle.

4-III-82

So much comes back now, even unbidden. I remember. Scared. Scared of all I'm feeling. I don't want to need you. You or anyone. Even with all the blood, I can shoulder it as my own brief miracle and loss. Yet I know that we are joined forever, somehow, by this too-brief juncture of our most precious living matter.

8-III-82

For the first time I have a voice. I write to you, *about* you and yet you are also a touchstone for other things, things I've always tried to say.

The blood is started up again. Rich, sudden flow and you so far away. I am angry and scared at not understanding these intimate functions and their irrational schedule. Doctor tomorrow again.

11-III-82

[*H*.: This was from a letter I wrote to Dan; remember, el Mr. Dicki, my good friend at Berkeley and la Trish's deep crush?]

Daniel: I think you know the latest from Trish, es decir, the chévere lie I made up to get out of six days of teaching to meet los boys in Houston and then go on to the Mardi Gras and Chicago. In Houston I conceived a baby with Mr. Montenegro, which then suddenly flooded out, rich and darkly, for three days. Finally, as Howard said, "the poor little bugger gave himself up for Lent." Seventy-two-hour spontaneous aborto, the doctor called it.

15-JJJ-82

These days are so much like an endless thread unravelling. Sometimes I can find a section of it, near the middle, and then the labyrinth paths reveal their contours with a clarity I can move within boldly. Other times, though this does not bring me to despair, there is simply too much material and I only see the end of the thread, tiny, fluttering far away. So, perhaps my writing becomes as Theseus's steps: errant, searching more than forging a definite path.

22-JJJ-82

Ah, my love. What really keeps me alive these days is remembering the sound of your laugh, your sultry and urgent Montenegro voice on the phone, the possibility of seeing and recording with my pen the beauty and horror of your land.

28-JJJ-82

My nightmares spring from my only worry lately, my massive bills [but how *could* they have been, really, oh, you poor girl! I was a graduate student; I barely even bought anything on credit . . . all I know is I was constantly worried about $]. Last night I awoke and I swear I *saw* you, right here next to me, saying, "Don't worry, my precious. It's all right. You won't have to work like that again; I'm here."

Anyway though, I want to ask: Have you gotten all the Chinese fortunes clipped together? I want to know *exactly* what is your response to all of these words [sound familiar?].

You ask about the blood. This is now the *third* issuing of blood in a month. The doctor explained that after a miscarriage the cycle may take several months to right itself. But I say to you, the answer is another. It is obvious to me, a woman with cycles regular as clockwork, that this crazily timed blood is responding to an entirely *different* calendar. This hormonal anarchy allegorizes my life, and so I don't worry. Montenegro, amor, it's simple: you have deregulated me.

2 - JU - 82

*O*h, H., such a letter I have never, *ever*. I, for whom correspondence is an integral part of my daily routine, my well-being [tru dat!] — what a beautiful letter you've sent me. ¡Coño! September is *so* far away.

Let us *never* stop writing, though. Even when we are together, let us never forget the time, *now*, when this epic flood of words was our homestead.

8 - JU - 82

*I*t is 4:30 a.m. I cannot sleep, and I *so* love sleep. Now that you are not here to share it with me, I sleep like an island at the center of my island bed, in my little room above Chestnut Street. I feel intensely the contour of my body against the too-cool sheets.

All these good things, so rich the pen cannot surround them and so I feel lost. My city is beautiful. I walk every day now, in the sun, alone. I want to know this place, these breathtakingly steep hills, these old, stately houses, before I leave. San Francisco is a city like no other.

Your card arrived today. The pictures are lovely. Don't worry, I forget nothing, *nothing*. I listen to my African animals tape in the shower [now *that* was devotion!]; I look at the photo of us kissing in the middle of the street, in New Orleans — *what* a kiss, you can see it in Ken's face — and my muscles and tendons flex to attention even now, now remembering the command of your hand on my thigh, knowing I can wrap all my weight into my legs, around your waist, and you will hold me, easy.

It is a wonder to me now, not a sadness, really, not a weight, that in that photo there was another inside me, with us. [Our little zygote, we called it, remember?]

15 - IV - 82

I lie here in bed and marvel at the swiftness of the mail from Cullinan. From Premier Diamond Mine, where you are now a mining engineer [I could scarcely picture this—you, underground—before moving to RSA, and just kept thinking of the poor canary!]. I marvel at your lucid, articulate, passionate prose. I lie in bed now, as the evening approaches yet the sky does not grow dark. It is a brilliant pale azure; the day is clear, as have been so many of these Thursdays. The 30-Stockton buses streak by below, I hear the *click click* of the electric sky rails that power them. Below is the street, the day, spring, life.

16 - IV - 82

It's Friday now. I've spoken to you. It's psychic how our missives so often overlap in content, in expression even, when I am sure you haven't read yet, at the moment of writing, that uncanny, similar phrasing in my letter.

P.S. Correct my Afrikaans, for Chrissake! And how the hell do you say "bend" or "fold"? Ah, that newspaper you sent depresses me. Can't make head or tails of that strange, garbled spelling. Carol dell'Amico [remember, my friend and former student at Berkeley; she lived for years in Port Elizabeth] says I *will* learn [and so I did, *net 'n bietjie*].

17 - IV - 82

*C*ousin Lee's birthday today. She's twenty-two. The darling Sloth, as we nicknamed her that time at "Hamburger Mary," remember, feels "terribly old." What I want now, more than anything, is for my vocation to become a fleshed-out reality. In these sunny spring San Francisco days I *live* for my writing, which brings me close to you.

"Start Me Up" on the turntable now. Our song. I'd pushed it to the back of the closet for a few days; it reminds me too much of you, of our Mardi Gras road trip. Raunchy, loud. You and I smile, a look of joyous rock 'n' roll mischief passes between us in the van. It is good, *so* good to be in our twenties, good to be alive and driving, smoking, making love. Talking about Petrarch, Eliot, Bob Dylan. Politics. Apartheid, Central America. Anything, everything! Sparring with you. Absolutely in love, for once, with a like soul [ah, I did feel *exactly* that then, so full and free; that charge returns now, reading, remembering].

24-V-82

[*Presies* twenty-six years later, to the day, I am typing this here.]

My mind aclutter—money's running out, as usual [lost my job as a Spanish T.A. at Berkeley that quarter, due to "cutbacks," remember? I was living on my savings. Vivid memory of having, at one terrifyingly low point, all of sixty dollars to my name]. I must get a moving truck and begin to dismantle this apartment. This one precious to me beyond any of the other temporary encampments of my past six- or seven-year gypsy trek—though just as temporary, really. Here has been a *home,* filled with memory and memorabilia. My walls echo with your low, beautiful voice, my pillow still holds your scent, my shower curtain pole is the curious resting place for your toothbrush, my espresso maker and penguin copulating mugs the homely vessels I served you with.

A gentle lucidity settles in this evening, like the lovely fog that descends now, cresting Fillmore Hill, cooling the too-hot concrete that has glistened all day in an unnatural-for-NoCal-coast swelter. Yes, it settles in and eases all this clutter.

I wonder where you are, Montenegro, mi vida. You, whose image surrounds me as I sit here on my island bed, amidst half-packed books and empty boxes. Your image, these *foties,* my only anchor in this sea of misplaced belongings and sadness. I always get sorrowful when I move. I should be used to it by now; I've averaged four to six moves a year for ages. I *have* been really a gypsy, you see; I know now it was all leading up to this, my final *voortrek* to your heart and home.

10-VJ-82

A strong California sun is a high yellow orb in cloudless sky. The fog of every Santa Cruz summer morning has burned off or been carried off by an unseasonable gusty breeze, which even now deflects and softens the steady heat without diminishing it somehow. It whistles through the miniature bamboo here on the redwood deck, brings the acrid geranium scent right up to my nostrils from the flower bed below, in the newly manicured backyard, sings in the pine trees, teases the woodpeckers in the maple oak, and purrs over the compact, gray-leaved bush whose name I can't recall or, more than likely, never knew.

I have lovely dreams about you that alternate with vivid nightmares provoked, I'm sure, by all my obsessive reading and thinking about your country.

My body toasts itself a nut-brown with only a few minutes of California sun a day [I was obliged to sunbathe; remember? Not that I needed much encouragement in those days, before global warming, before we had SPF's and knew the evils of tanning. . . . I'd contracted hepatitis and was so, so sick. My parents secretly hoped being skinny and weak and jaundiced would put me off my move to your country, pero no such animal!]. The miracle of my race, this hybrid that would be classified "coloured" in your country, I think, is that the pale-limbed, green-eyed, chestnut-tressed Siberian gives way in the sun—no problem—to the smooth, honey-gold flesh that is the Mexican in me. I am my father's daughter in the winter, my mother's in the summer. Simple [um, *hardly*!].

28-VJ-82

*H*oward. I have written your name so many times in these past months—five now, exactly, since we met—countless times. Sending you clippings [ah, I *still* love to do this, snail-mail girl at heart!], wondering what you're doing, if you think of me obsessively in your waking and sleeping hours, as I do you?

I am seized with fear when I contemplate the enormous changes I face. Geography, people, laws, apartheid. And yet you know me. I falter not. It is (as Cortázar remarked about me) *always* curiosity—it overpowers my fear of the unknown—that drives me, spurs my heels, licks at my heart like flames. I am so happy. I have never been happier.

29-VI-82

*H*oward, you are learning, I trust (if you didn't know it from the moment we met, as soon as we began to talk!) that my convictions run deep, as deep as my heritage. An amalgam I am, a blueprint of the triumphs and tragedies of this hardy mongrel breed [wow, strange, prescient, my use of this *very* controversial, contested, and contestatory term, *nê?*].

I tell you this not to antagonize you, for I believe you and I are on the same side, though our circumstances seem to conspire to widen the gulf between us.

[*Ag*, and this was *precisely* what happened, what I *felt* happening from the moment I pitched up in your country. We allowed it to happen. Why did we allow ourselves to founder—come to ground, eventually— on this twinned reef: the untenable reality of apartheid—the way it infiltrated every tiny crevice of daily life and poisoned it—*and* my guilt and anger, projected like a heat-seeking missile toward your heart, about having gone to live with/in it? *Why* didn't you fight for me? Why didn't we fight harder for our love?]

I tell you of these things so you may more fully comprehend what moving to South Africa represents to me: *it goes against every fiber of my being*. Yet I have said—and I remain adamant—I *shall* not do without you.

I'm feeling lost now. Scared [the thought of not having a job to go to unnerved me; I'd *never* not worked, since I was fifteen or sixteen].

There's no Spanish department at your fucking university, Wits, nor at any of the others I've written to. They want me to teach French, for Chrissake, or Portuguese, or Italian! That's rich, as you'd say. But, inasmuch as this is all I *can* do at present, I offer myself to you as a woman who will love you, fully [did you know, *really* know, how much?]. I have not realized myself yet. It will take time, and I'll need you, your love, your support. I am a writer. *This* is first and foremost who I am.

[H.: those were the last words of this book; two months later I was in South Africa.]

V

In My Country Crónica

12 July 2005
Los Angeles

For Wim Lindeque, Melanie "Miss Mellie" Maree, and
Shaun Levin, y
para Eunice Van Wagner Chávez, in memoriam

Afrikaans words and phrases insinuate themselves into my head, my consciousness, aun sin querer. *Meer en meer.* Not sure I even *want* them in there, *presies,* although tengo que admitir they do stir something in me. Algo del orden de (*pace* Andrea Gutiérrez, your fave phrase, o al menos, *one* of them) la añoranza. *Yebo*: longing, comfort, long-ago pain. Memory.

Of my self hace años, en Pretoria. Después de casi un año, a year of holding myself apart, gingerly beginning to let the words—and those who spoke them from birth—touch me, assuage the biting loneliness. *Kom ons jol! Ag, nee man. Lekker,* my china.

Still not sure about—hasta ahora, desde aquí, después de todos estos años and even with all this reading, these movies, trying to prepare myself, somehow, for my return, mi iminente retorno a Sudáfrica, después de veinte años—my relationship to that *taal*.

Hace unos días, more terrorist bombings. En Londres. Impotencia. Miedo. *Ons kannie* anywhere trek anymore *nie,* it seems. Last night I watched John Boorman's film *In My Country*. Basado en ese libro, which I haven't found yet, but which that girl told me to read, esa niña que había estado de study abroad in South Africa, cuando fui a leer en la University of Redlands, invitada por mi amiga la Eva Valle. Anygüey, *julle,* you know the *boek* I'm talking about, *The Country of My Skull* (weird title: Pierre *dixit,* claro que es adrede, pero it sounds pirate-y to me, not poetic) by Antjie Krog. The movie was sappy, a bit Manichean, pero all things considered, not bad.

And you know me, anygüey; for so many years the slightest reference to Suid-Afrika, just the slightest mention, and I'd get teary, nostalgic, or angry: I was there. I *lived* there. I know that place. When did that *reaksie* change? Was it when I began to embrace my Latinidad, con ahinco, en serio, for reals, como quien dice? My self en relación a mi Latinidad, a California, Los Angeles, to a feeling of home, belonging, en vez de mi yo, for years siempre flotante, unmoored and always, *always* en relación al Africa?

Oh, why did I leave? And was it right to come back here, a Califas, to come home? *Is* this home?

Pero anygüey, volviendo al film, sentí una immediate—y al principio inexplicable—repugnancia atroz toward the character played by el Samuel L. Jackson. Pero luego it hit me: *that* was precisely how I felt and acted when I first pitched up in South Africa. Shit, and I'm not even *noire*! Y bueno, antes, en la universidad, en la graduate school, even in high school: oh, little Miss Divestment, little Miss Anti-Apartheid activista. Miss Marxista.

Al nada más llegar, eché la culpa de cuarenta años de historia on Howard, en su familia. But especially on him. He never had a chance. *We*
never had a chance! No en ese país, en su país. So righteous, tan supe-
rior porque nunca había tenido una empleada doméstica. Never had a
maid (a *meid*). If you get right down to it, rompí con Howard, essentially, porque no podía bregar con la gran culpabilidad que sentí. My
guilt. It overwhelmed me como una ola: sudden, relentless, nauseating.

From the minute my feet hit the tarmac at Jan Smuts International airport, en agosto del '82, it hit me: el peso de la culpabilidad, of whiteness,
y de todo lo que ese whiteness implicaba en Sudáfrica. Porque *that's* the
way I was read there: como blanca. En la paranoia taxonómica del apartheid, no había modo de leer a una Chicana. And besides, bueno, let's
face it: casi nunca me reconocen como raza, not even in the good ol'
U.S.A. Anygüey, la cosa es que I couldn't get out from under it. Couldn't
stay with a white, South African man (no matter how gorgeous, intelligent, passionate, sexy, and trilingüe; no matter that I was in love: I
couldn't get past, no podía bregar con su blancura) and ride that wave.

Pero vaya arrogancia. What assumptions. *Ag*, I feel *such* retroactive
self-loathing now, después de ver ese film, for the way I was then: intransigente, smug. Seeing *myself* now in Samuel Jackson's periodista. A
white-skinned, Jewish, brown Mexi-girl whose skin could not be read
"properly" en ese país and so, para que los Afrikaners y los ingleses no
me pensaran uno de ellos, I kept myself apart: insular yet achingly
lonely 24/7, angry, accusatory, and aloof. My *own* private apartheid del
corazón.

It was only my innate, insatiable curiosidad (linguistic, cultural,
social)—y el que mi amigo negro, Mmome Neppe Selabe, who worked
in the photocopying department at UNISA (la University of South Africa, donde, against all odds, encontré trabajo), me dijera, "Oh, *come
on Suzi, you've *got* to learn their language, girl. To understand them. To
understand all of us!"—que finalmente me indujo hacia el deshielo. To
begin, grudgingly, tentative, to thaw. To listen. To speak.

Oh, Wim, *you* helped me melt then, you helped me relearn laughter, how to be alive. You who grew up entre *Engels* y Afrikaner, me enseñaste a negociar con las posibilidades—and the limitations—de lo que podíamos hacer. *Om te speel,* even! Entonces. Oh, Father (you, un cura católico ahora: adiós Mr. Polisie, *tot siens,* bifeliz party *boytjie,* hey?), forgive me now. Bless me. Ayúdame a perdonar(me) . . .

Ah, but I *did* learn (didn't I?). Ese learning que sólo viene de vivir en un lugar. Conocer. Living in and among. Los pactos, la rabia e impotencia y el júbilo diarios. Seeing. Writing.

Such shame and anger, de repente, at myself. De nuevo. *Just* like twenty years ago and just from a movie! Ay, cómo eres susceptible. Pierre me dijo: no te odies tanto. You need your *own* Truth and Reconciliation Commission, niña.

Hot tears coursing; I cringe, al escuchar los (after all only) skin-deep, righteous, outraged pronouncements del suddenly *so* glaringly American Sam Jackson, as the African American reportero del *Washington Post* at the TRC hearings. Mientras tanto los otros, los non-hyphenated africanos—Africans a secas, or South Africans black, white, and coloured—try to explain to him, to show him, to make him understand *ubuntu*: forgiveness. Interconnectedness.

Ay, ya sé que it's only a movie. Pero still, there's a knot inside me, este nudo a *need* to be there again. Ahora, *nou-nou,* hot tears spilling onto that airport tarmac, onto that red *rooi* roja tierra. I want to apologize (¿por mi presencia? for my absence?). Quiero agradecer.

I know so much *less* now, a veces pienso. And yet, I feel even more, si cabe (yet so much more ambiguously), than ever before.

Mi Agüela Eunice, tras un fulminante debate entre life and death, falleció hace dos días. I let her go; me despedí de ella. Estuve con ella, not like with Daddy, ni con mamá. Mi hijo Etienne está lejos. Oh, I want to fuzz his hair, look into his almond-shaped dark eyes, see them, see me seeing him in them, ojalá fueran sus ojos no nublados de rabia,

56

resentimiento. What I miss isn't here any more. Isn't *him* any more (bueno, OB-vio). Oh my God, parezco esa canción "Los recuerdos no abrazan," bien sappy y completely oxymoronic de Luciano "El Pibe de Luján" Pereyra.

That's what I want. Estar . . . allí, de nuevo. Or, patrás al futuro. Hoping we can be . . . *algo,* juntos. *Saam.* Again.

Tengo miedo. Stomach a knot of apprehension, nausea, no puedo comer, duermo pésimo. What will the new South Africa feel like? What will you be like? What will we *all* be like, together again? Pero I'm dreaming about you, Wimmie en Mellie. My *skatties,* so far away pero ever closer. Pronto, pronto. *Julle* en Afrika, my Suid-Afrika, every night. *Goeie naand.*

VI

San Francisco Days Crónica

20 May 2008
Saratoga, CA

For Bethany-Rachel Bentley and Suzinn "Lee" Weiss, and
for Chris Isaak, por tu voz

Yesterday I drove up to San Francisco en la espuela del momento with la Cronopia Raz. You're not gonna believe this. La Cronopia had invited me over to her pad (literally, she lives like a quarter of a mile del Montalvo) para acompañarla en un health walk, and then we were slated to have luncheon after. Llevé un sencisho change of clothes with me (velveteen *noir* pants, you know, como un tracksuit bottom, pero w/ T-shirt, OB-vio, *not* a matching velveteen hoodie, pa' no dar la impresión de ser una de esas Valley Girl, Juicy Couture chix! CHALE to that!), and my fuchsia and orange Croc slides.

Well, de repente me pregunta si me apetece drive up to S.F. with her, just like that! So, quién soy yo pa' look a gift drive en la boca, right? You know how much I love los spontaneous road trips. La Cronopia es muy striking, altísima, con un super shiny, chocolate-colored bob. Greek (American). Bien eccéntrica, espontánea y lively. A Scorpio. Drives a pearlescent white Acura con sunroof and she can do a *gull* of things at the same time: escuchar música on a winkie wankie, change the songs about a zillion times (la mejor fue some sort of dance number, bien electronic, con el John Malkovich entoning las inmortales palabras "It's beyond my control," you know, de *Dangerous Liaisons*. Simply *troppo*!), open and close el sunroof, type directions into this little box que habla con disembodied voz de una mujer on Thorazine. Bueno, and DRIVE, OB-vio. *Quite* well. Bien skilled, just like you, Lee. You and your New Jersey skills. Una total multitasker. Ja ja, not me!

Por un momento estuve a punto de decirle: No way, look how I'm dressed, I'm all sweaty, and besides, I have to write. Pero luego lo pensé mejor. Like, why did I have to be so staunch about trying to force myself back into my glass-walled cubicle, if, after all, San Francisco has thus far been one of my *main* sites, actually el ür-site, de mi inspiración? Right? So, nos juimos.

Oh, those lion-colored hills de ambos lados de la 280N make me weep, ecstatically, con su belleza. Y hasta comencé a sentir un odd, grudging, nostalgic fondness por estos ridículos, sketchy, erratic NoCal conductores. Las asiáticas dolled up to the nines al volante de sus Mercs y Lexi, con sus trendy, retro bubble peinados and even *bigger* bubble designer gafas de sol. Damn, patrás a los '80s, no shit. Los Corvette-wielding, slide right up on your nalga, dot-com hotdoggers.

Well, como sabes, there's S.F. y S.F. La Cronopia y yo, siguiendo las melífluas instrucciones de esa talking chick en su GPS (ella me explicó que así se llama ese chismecito, you know me . . . aparento ser techno-clueless, pero really, agarro la onda right away cuando quiero), first drove down through the Presidio, skirted the Marina, y terminamos en Fort Mason, en ese famoso gourmet reataurante vegetariano called Greens. You would've enJOYed. We had luncheon, y luego volvimos por la Marina to North Beach.

En otras palabras, my old haunts, precisamente. You remember que la Marina is where I was living con la Trish, on Chestnut Street, cuando conocí a Howard en el Balboa Café. I hadn't often been back in that barrio, en los años después de regresar de South Africa, because la Pamela W. y su business partner y roomie el Robbie Marks, and all my other friends in S.F. (of which tragically, as you know, *none* remain any more), se habían mudado a otros barrios.

Con la Cronopia, we drove (quite by accident, or fortuitously) *all* thru my old neighborhoods, tanto Chestnut como Van Ness (donde había vivido con Mauro Ritucci, before Howard, *ti ricordi*?). Parqueamos y entramos a un Italian café on Columbus, near the one you and I used to love, remember? Caffe Puccini? El vato behind the counter se parecía al David Román; he was *abbastanza* simpático, in a laconic, slightly wary way. Pero entonces this larger dude, bien capo, hair *very* engominado, entró y comenzaron a platicar in rapid-fire, regional code-switching. It was *fantastic*. It seemed to me a Sicilian, o al menos southern, dialect, intercut with splashes of perfect English. *Molto* hand-waving.

I felt transported suddenly, out of time. Through the "time tunnel" (remember ese TV show que me fascinaba de niña? Where these two very homosocial *okes* kind of . . . entran a una máquina, y son transportados a otras épocas, like Ancient Rome, or the Titanic? P. ordered it on Netflix, pero trágicamente, resultó que es *bien* dated y camp, not at *all* mysterious or high tech, como me había parecido, as a child). Pero anygüey, sentada en ese café, me sentí repentinamente patrás, back to the days cuando volvía a casa en el BART, home to the City from Berkeley, after teaching my classes, y esperaba en varios North Beach cafes y bares para que Mauro saliera del *lavoro*.

Así fue como aprendí a hablar italiano: by sitting around in North Beach, corrigiendo ensayos estudiantiles, tomando café, fumando Gauloises, listening to Italians talk. *Va be'*, of course, *also* by being thrown into the deep end (or diving in): moving *in* with one, a Pasolini-reading intellectual de Foligno, cuyo inglés, cuando yo lo conocí, was so limited he actually asked me why, en una, such an inexplicably *large* amount of salt was sold in the U.S. (due to "sale" signs in shop windows!). Te lo juro, that's the truth!

Bueno, esos vatos del café nos estaban none too subtly checking out a la Cronopia y a mí. Trying to figure out de dónde éramos, since, como sabes, la gente quite often mistake me for Italian, y la Cronopia is—and looks—Greek. As we waltzed outta there, I cheerfully looked "il Capo" in the eye y le dije, "*Ciao bello, grazie!*" Cronopia gave them una mirada silent but drop-dead sexy. It was amusing in extremis.

Volvimos entonces al Acura, parked right near the Saints Peter and Paul Catholic Church (al lado del Washington Square Park), donde asistí a una boda, italianísima. OB-vio, with Mauro. Ay, esa combinación de roasting coffee, las cadencias de chino e italiano in the air, the icy, harsh May wind que azotaba el ridículo, puce-green men's wool sweater que me había prestado la Cronopia, to throw over my almost–leisure suit atuendo (probably the *weirdest* outfit I've ever worn—digo, sin querer—in San Francisco), the less than 60 degree weather. Ah, it was too much. Demasiado. *Troppo.*

My heart a fragile pincushion, como los que vi en los tourist shops en la Grant Avenue last summer, cuando estuve en Chinatown con Pierre y Wim. Donde compré ese amethyst crystal from that chévere, butchy china, who insisted it was for me (cuando se lo quería comprar a la B-2). "No, for you, for *you*. Protection. Take bad things out of body." It hangs on my espejo retrovisor now.

I felt porous, persimmon-squishy, light. Permeable. Flotante. Dangerously abierta. *Too* open to the past. To the pinprick wounds del pasado. Assailed, both by the timeless belleza de North Beach (OK, sólo *almost* timeless, pero al menos North Beach parece cambiar slower than the rest of the city) y por los recuerdos. I had to fight hard, de repente, to keep the smarting tears from my eyes, pa' que la Cronopia no me pensara directamente loca. Bueno, maybe I *am* . . .

Oh well, ni modo. Let's just say, *alla fine,* que ayer fue un día *bien* Mercury in Pisces, en la casa tres.

Un Pico (De)presión
Diptych

VII

Trincheras Crónica

26 julio 2004
Los Angeles

Para Lucía "Lucy War" Guerra Cunningham y
Adelaida López-Mejía

Me tengo que fortalecer, somehow, para outlast him. Al Juvenil.
Pero, *how*? No entiendo cómo estas mujeres, by their own admission
dañadas, vulnerables (como la abandonada-by-teen-mom, rail-thin, in-
cest survivor, la lovely, mega-talentosa icy blonde Kathryn Harrison,
por ejemplo), can be mothers. No me cabe en la cabeza. And not only
mothers (y la Harrison tiene *tres,* coño) sino writers too. O quizás hasta
writers, sobre todo. Si a mí, apenitas puedo, al parecer, *barely* keep my
head above water. I'm drowning con sólo uno.

Mi amiga Adelaida (who doesn't have kids pero posee unos recuerdos
uncannily nítidos de su propia adolescencia, de cómo torturaba a su
mamá in three-hour, protracted verbal arañazo-fests) me dice que she's

heard that living with an adolescent es como tener un enemigo en casa.
¡Simón! Pero esa expression es tan trillada that it just doesn't even begin
to get at "the horror, the horror" (ay, speaking of *Apocalypse Now*: ¡Pobre
Brando! Fellow Aries. And what a bizarre, torturous vida familiar. Esos
kids! Q.E.P.D.).

Y el horror de esa enmity, que se banaliza en la redundancia discur-
siva, resides precisely en su literalidad. Living with the enemy—con *mi*
enemigo/mi Juvenil, anyway—significa tener el cuerpo en un constant
state of fight-or-vuelo arousal (este hecho dificulta, amortigua—ah, let's
just spit it out—directamente *troncha,* dicho sea de paso, otros tipos de
arousal . . .).

Pero anygüey, como les estaba diciendo, este estar siempre vigilante, always on edge, is doing me *in,* carnales. I can't put it any other way than
these absolutely unoriginal, *Woman's Day* and *Good Housekeeping* ex-
presiones. Vagas. Universales. Trivializantes, somehow. Pero trust me:
I—*yo,* aquí en ésta *mi* vida—am in hell.

I feel like la plaga. Mis amigos, muchos de ellos, me esquivan (well,
who wouldn't? Parezco broken record, joder). Creo que they think it's
catching. Que mi hostil, hotheaded, fuera-de-control Juvenil will rub
off on their kid. Or that my hyperbolic desperation, mi creciente nega-
tividad, my eroding esperanza para EL FUTURO will infect them.

Me siento awkward. Huraña. A la vez, I need help pero no sé cómo
pedir without sounding pathetic. Like a candidate for Thorazine . . . o,
al menos, Oprah. Debe haber algún modo, some way to get through
this. There *must.* La gente habla de fases, stages, túneles. De alternating
moments, periods. Light and dark. Debe haber un modo. Simplemente
hunker down, me digo. Do my own thing, tener mi propia vida, mis
"propios intereses." Algo que le indique al Juvenil—sin lugar a dudas—
que I have my own life, que estoy viva, coño. Que I have my *own* life, y
no existo sólo in relation to y para él.

How to loosen this unhealthy knot que él desprecia pero a la vez exige?
Me siento, against my will, como el hermoso, doomed Jeremy Planchas

y su identical twin (also played by el prodigiosamente talentoso Planchas, OB-vio), su doppelgänger in Cronenberg's *Dead Ringers*. Yo y el Juvenil. Joey and I. I was always *so* proud—hasta smug—about our closeness. Pues parece death grip now. Yeah, locked in a death dance con alguien que es, at the same time, as remote and impassive as the moon. "I'm *dyin'* in here," como se quejó el Al Pacino as Sonny in *Dog Day Afternoon*. Acosada. Suffocating.

At what cost to me if I remain with him en este tango enfermizo? Pero, ¿y qué choice tengo? Faltan seis meses pa' que cumpla los dieciocho años. El año (c)académico ni siquiera comienza—falta un mes—and already I feel restless, fuzzy, unfocused, and like I'm sinking sloooowly, como ese res, creo que fue (¿capaz un cabasho?) en la novela *Doña Bárbara*, que se metió en el tremedal. Ooh, I love that word! La aprendí con la Lucy War hace un chingo de años, en su clase sobre la novela hispanoamericana. Anygüey, like I was saying, lentamente, agonizingly esa bestia was sucked under that quicksand, bramando pitifully, eyes rolling.

Pero, y . . . (pausa porteña) ehperá un momento, muñeca. Suddenly la anagnórisis hits me, plain as the (alas, algo demasiado pronounced) nariz on my face: maybe *herein* lies la salvación. Words. Las palabras siempre me han salvado. Han postergado, al menos, my absolute collapse. Y quizás this is as close to salvation as I'll ever get.

Novelas. Las devoro. Vidas ajenas, sometimes *muy* ajenas. Or, uneasily semejantes a la mía. Marianne Wiggins's strange—no matter how many times I reread it—ominous, dreamy *John Dollar*. W. H. Hudson's classic (bueno, algo camp a estas alturas, hay que admitirlo) *Green Mansions*. Diana Bellessi's latest poetry. Y toda la noche, hace tres noches cuando el Juvenil no regresaba y no regresaba a casa, all night long I read *What I Loved*, por la incomparablemente misteriosa Siri Hustvedt. Finished it in six and a half hours. I'm hard to peg. Estoy all over the place, sha lo sé. Leo voraz, constante y promiscuamente.

And even more than my—these days near obsessional—devouring of words, la salvación está en esto: my feverish *scratch scratch scratching* of rust-colored, fat, felt-tip pen. ¡He aquí! Con este acto puedo—*tengo* que—expiar, extirpar la angustia. Mitigar. Paliar. What else to do? I can't run away de la maternidad. So, no me queda otra. Escribir.

Justo cuando temía que it was gone. All dried up, shriveled como el scorched chaparral aquí en el Evil, que digamos el *Inland*, el Imperio del Interior, después de los wild fires last fall. Gone, gone, pa' nunca regresar (ay, *such* a drama queen). Carcomida, wrung out por una galloping ansiedad (*anguhtia,* they'd correct me, en Buenos Aires) that not all the Pilates and yoga and Xanax en el mundo can attenuate. Can even begin to make a dent in.

Pero de repente I am seized. Hace un calor infernal afuera. The A/C is already cycling *on/off, on/off* y son apenas las 10 a.m. But I have to, *have* to fall to the pale toffee-colored, sisal-look moqueta que instalamos al volver de la Argentina three long summers ago (everything en este modest condo I call home de golpe se ve nítido, hasta hermoso, technicolor coordinated, armonioso). I *have* to grab my diario and my pen y las palabras, como siempre—digo, OK, en mis momentos más sublimes—just *come*. Unbidden. They course through me y yo, al parecer, sólo las transmito.

Ya sé que esta teoría romántica—poet as medium, y bla bla—está *waaaay* out of fashion. So pre-PoMo es casi ridículo. Pero ni modo. For now, it works for me, como quien dice. Works for me.

VIII

Hawk Call Crónica

10 July 2007
Claremont, Califas

For Pierre
and for Etienne, con esperanza

Yahrzeit Agüela, Q.E.P.D.

Esta mañana, I saw a pair of hawks. No. Primero los escuché: their wild, Native American, shrill calls punzaron la semi-calma de otra anodyne mañana en el Evil. El Inland Empire de Califas. Digo semi-calma porque hace semanas que I'm daily assailed by a sense of dread. La definición misma de la anguhtia. Is this "generalized anxiety disorder," ¿o alguna forma menor, más suave?

Ni modo. Whatever it's called, I *have* it. No hay razón, uno diría. Pero its very unreason es la naturaleza de la bestia. A sense of foreboding dogging me, always already (*pace* Derrida) detached, severed from—y anterior a—cualquier fuente reconocible.

Salí al patio para regar. Weirdly, there was a close, dense gray, southern sky. Como si estuviéramos, instead, en Charleston. Or, why not, en Buenos Aires en febrero. Arriba, en las ramas bajas del enorme pine tree, justo al otro lado del fence, I caught the flash of plump, downy-white avian nalgas, the powerful black-speckled gray plumes of flecha-straight tail feathers. They moved among the branches; they fluttered and screeched and wheeled. Definitely halcones de algún tipo. Red-tailed hawks? I've always loved them. Sort of feared them, también, aunque casi siempre se les ve way up en el aire, a swooping dark speck, al lado de la Highway 101, por ejemplo, on any south-to-north Califas road trip.

Pero hoy, I *saw* them. Clear and close. Garras, picos, powerful wings. One soared to an adjacent eucalyptus, pero como que no le daba suficiente shelter. It circled, volvió al pino, and settled in again, calling to the other one all the while. In dizzyingly close detalle los observé. Tan wild, tan próximos al predecible humdrumness de mi pequeño patio suburbano.

Suddenly, del otro lado del gate, por una ranura vertical, there was an eye: its gaze met mine. Se me cayó la garden hose de la mano. It was five, maybe even eight seconds, se me hace, before I recognized la pupila, strangely small and hard para la too-soft (for SoCal) morning light: el Juvenil.

Me sentí curiosamente detached, flotante. Se me ocurrió que esa pareja de hawks was you and me: solitarios, together. Criaturas ariscas que, sin embargo, nest together. Never quite retracting del todo las garras. Primed and ready, para en cualquier momento despellejar al enemigo. Any interloper. We are inward, insular, en estos días, heart(h)bound. More fiercely self-protective than ever, parece . . .

I used to think I would do *anything* para el Juvenil. The line from that Irish movie, *Cal,* remember, cuando el John Lynch le pregunta a la Kate Nelligan (or, coño, it's gone fuzzy on me: was it Helen Mirren? You'd think I'd remember, la Helen *is* one of my all-time faves, after all, mientras que la Kate barely registers en mi al menos used-to-be memoria de elefante. My only clear memory of her is in that ridiculous, over-the-top spy movie con el Donald Sutherland, when he drops down onto his knees, al final, on some tarmac, y creo que la Kate de repente le mata de un balazo, this incongruously climactic moment capping a wannabe tumultuous, passionate romance. Pero cuando lo vi con mis padres, ese film—*Eye of the Needle,* el título, suddenly returns to me—in the Nickelodeon Theatre, en Santa Cruz, y con mi prima la Lee Weiss, we all had *such* a fit of hueso-rattling risa at that tarmac-shooting moment, cuando los demás moviegoers estaban hasta teary-eyed, we were almost ejected del teatro. Uf, pero sorry for derailment, esa es otra): anygüey, el John Lynch character's line en el film *Cal* was "Would you die for me?"

Siempre me pareció swooningly romantic, pero adaptable, de todos modos. A semaphore, a floating signifier of fierce passion. De pareja, o de madre. Either one.

Pero ahora sé que no. He aprendido que no. No, I wouldn't. "Just say no"; he aprendido esta lección. Que Tough Love por acá, que charlas con la Claremont police por allá. I've learned that my "anything," al menos, comes with strings attached. Tipo, *if you're ready to start studying again, then we'll* . . . Or, *si realmente quieres encontrar donde vivir, te* . . . Y así. Porque ¿de qué serviría que yo fuera al edge with him, and right *over,* si a la vez me hundo a mí misma? Right?

Soy empedernida edge-dweller, though. Al borde de. Abrazada al acantilado, pero . . . y no.

You know. Teeter-tottering por la maternidad y por la vida: esa soy yo. Still. Siempre.

IX

Oda a la Ambigüedad Crónica

11 febrero 2006
Claramonte, Califas

Para Paul Allatson y
para David William "el Noviete" Foster

*P*ensé, por un momento eterno, que me habías perdido, que te había perdido. That we'd lost each other. ¿Cuánto tiempo without words, without even a glimpse? How could we go that long without?

Después de un torrential exchange que sólo ahora me vengo a dar plena cuenta de que you rely upon like nourishment. Me lo dices en tu carta, pero antes, en otra carta, once upon a time, lo repudiaste, as excessive. Desconcertante.

Waves of alivio wash over me, ahora que nos hemos permitido honrar, decir las palabras vedadas. Pronunciamos palabras como closeness, miedo, daring, almas gemelas. Bueno, en realidad, souls *bien* different, pero touching. We tread, gingerly, por territorios no cartografiados.

Te permites (some dam broke in you—un límite traspasado—el otro día, and I am grateful, me siento reivindicada) . . . you allow yourself the luxury of recognizing love. Sencillamente esto: el reconocimiento, sin acusarlo de desviarte. Aun en esta, una forma antes desconocida.

Camino rápido por esta sudden, too-early primavera. A small, icy rivulet of sweat runs down my spine. My tissue-weight turquoise cotton top se me pega, cual ventosa, a la piel, semi-transparentándose. My lips part slightly; tiny casi jadeos se me escapan. Voy bien rápido, long limbed. Y hace un calor intenso, unnatural en este supposedly still invernal Aquarius birthday season.

Un atroz rottweiler, slightly overweight, compact and dense as a rhino, me aborda, pegado a su equally chunky dueño. Me recuerda (*me hace acordar*, as they say en Buenos Aires), por un momento, el film *Doggy Love*, you know, con Gael García Bernal. Toda esa flashy, desperate, gritty mexicanidad. I watched it voluptuously, yearningly, en ese cine en Buenos Aires. Suddenly missing, visceralmente, the smells, the sounds of home. Digo, de mi *otro* hogar.

Pero really, apenas veo al rottweiler, de reojo. Camino tan rápido, casi estoy corriendo. And besides, you know me: mucho más mío es el olfato.

Blooming antes de tiempo, a deshora, las fuzzy mimosa blossoms despiden su pale, dusty yellow perfume. Me saltan las lágrimas de repente, unbidden, casi inappropriate, even, on this blindingly hot, clear midwinter day: how long since I've been home?

Marcos y Sara me platicaron el otro día de Santa Cruz, and they may as well have been talking about Mars. Ya no está mamá, my last link to home. No es mío, ya no es mi lugar en el mundo.

Pero the mimosa branches used to cool my lazy afternoon walks, de vuelta a casa de la high school. *Whoosh, whoosh.* Soplaban en la brisa marítima. The eucalyptus scattered their pods; occasionally a seagull would venture the quarter mile inland, y graznaba overhead mientras yo volvía a casa, avoiding huge, scary dogs, componiendo overwrought poems en la cabeza.

Camino, ahora. I reach up, overhead, and crush tiny red pirul berries. El Paulie cree que son native to Australia. Yeah right, as *if*! OB-vio, son una introduced species. Bueno, la verdad, I might've thought they were nativos a Califas, si no los hubiese visto, originally, en México. Ahora agarro una rama frondosa de delgadas, pálidas hojas. I rub them between my fingers—oh, la pimentosa oscura fragancia—y estoy en Zapopan, en verano.

La última vez que estuve en Guadalajara—almost ten years ago, can it be?—iba con el "Noviete" Foster, el conocidísimo hispanista y porteñófilo *sine qua non*. Anygüey, íbamos en taxi y él platicándome de la Pizarnik y sus amores. Y nomás circulamos por donde *era,* donde *había sido* mi barrio, y yo llorando por todo lo que se había ido. For everything I'd lost, por todo lo que ya no era. You know. Lo de siempre . . .

Ay, no puedo, no debo seguir así, rememorando. Tendré que llorar; it's going to slow me down, y necesito sudar, extenuarme, para volver a casa apacible, focused, para escribir.

Pero estos olores son too much. *Te veel,* como dice el OomBie. No puedo no estar en otros lugares, (mis) otros lugares. Tan faraway, tan míos, en mí, still. Siempre. Reactivados, reactualized by this or that scent. Repentino, site-specific, preciso como bala al corazón.

One of those places is (with) you.

Ecologically speaking (y LITTLE EYE, lo soy: reciclo, hasta compro scratchy Kleenex y todo), este definite sign of global warming, este premature heat, debería tenerme alarmada, en el infierno. Y me choca el calor anygüey; tú lo sabes. Sufro, quiero estar sólo adentro, moss green homemade velvet curtains drawn, fingiendo ser vampiresa. Escribiendo.

Pero speaking from the heart—y antes de que comience el true, searing, Imperio del Interior summer blast furnace, allí por agosto, septiembre—right here, right now estoy en el cielo. Y ¿sabes qué? Aquí me quedo, for now.

X

Mountainess/Montañ(os)a Crónica

5 mayo 2008
Montalvo Arts Center
Saratoga, Califas

For Tim Miller and
for Juan Carlos Galeano

I slept pretty well last night, my first night here en el Montalvo Arts Center (sola), because Pierre insisted I get a friggin' squishy, almost hongo-like memoria-foam mattress topper to improve on the bed-o'-nails feel of the mattress they provide. Bueno, it helped.

The repair *oke,* Steve, came over this morning, perceived the unlockable condición of the upstairs studio sliding-glass puerta and later—su palabra—"fiddled" with the lock un chingo y finalmente proudly announced que le echó un lubricante (?). Pero all his fiddlin' ended up being for naught: en cuanto saqué la llave, la puerta just slid right open again.

El tal Steve bears more than a passing resemblance to Texan *cantautor* Steve Earle, BTW. Me echó un solemne discurso sobre los mountain lions (aka cougar, puma, panther)! First off, me dijo que hay que respetar a la naturaleza, and to only do what you feel comfortable doing. And to mos def not hike ALONE, and to stay near people, on marked trails, etc. Bueno, OB-vio. But today, there seems to be basically no one en los trails. A bunch of little school kiddies up on the lawns at the villa (now *they'd* be tasty morsels, ¿qué no?) with some officious, print-frocked, oversized, probably designer sun gafa-ed, chupamedias, Stepford-looking teachers shrieking at them, "Line, I *said* LINE . . . ," as the littlies scattered erratically, shouting and squealing.

Anygüey, el Steve further informed me que según él, the best way to enter el bosque (or vohquie, *pace* Lemebel!) is with a .457 Magnum elephant gun. After I told him I'd lived in Africa, pronunció, "Well then, I'm preachin' to the choir." Um, *not*. Pero ni modo. I took his point.

Currently, he has temporarily abandoned ministrations to the writing-nook door. Tendré que insistir: *That* is where I want to write—es como si hubiesen construido el little crow's nest justo para mí—y no puedo, I can't leave my (Pomona College–owned, a fin de cuentas) MacBook Pro up there if it can't be locked! Pero he's now fishing about en el baño, since I had the *most* unpleasant experience, cuando finalmente me duché esta mañana, of emerging to an entirely puddled floor. When I, siempre science-minded, como saben, turned on the ducha again—this time standing *outside* para observar el water flow—vi que salía un atroh spray, out of the muy flimsily put together, supposedly hand-holdable shower.

QUEJA INTERRUPTA:

Talk about rasquache CENTRAL! You can't even take the handheld showerhead off and actually *hold* it in your hand, to luxuriate en una Euro-style ducha, pues está fixed, held fast in its tracks, by an elaborate wrap of hot pink cellophane that looks like nothing so much as a condom (el Steve estaba muy de acuerdo con mi descripción, FYI).

Anygüey, it was spraying out right there, de esa especie de joint, or joist, o como coño se llame, you know, that gasketlike thingie. Bueno, a blast of agua came out all horizontal, shot past the shower curtain (or *through,* for all I know, it's a dead-cheap, thin, annoyingly billowing white thing . . .), and even drenched the little IKEA-ish (por suerte es de metal) cabinet donde guardé mi makeup y mis remedios! Can you imagine? The horror, the horror!

I snatched up my precious little plastic thirty-seven-cent fruit-print travel case que compré hace mil años en el Cost Plus de San Francisco (que ya—disco rallado, ya lo sé—ni siquiera existe anymore), con todas mis pahtishas, etc., and rushed it outta there to dry land. Fixate yourself que habría directamente *matado* al tal Steve, o a la Julie, la residency manager, if anything aquatic had happened to my remedies! Or, God forbid, to my new Nars sombras, recently purchased from Sephora in tasteful, Wiggue-like shades of sand and taupe that I thought would be just the ticket for this bucolic artist-in-residency Retrete. Apropos of . . . bueno, de *nada,* exactly—excepto quizás el predecible, cíclico resurgimiento de mi fijación en el Africa—creo recordar que el eye shadow duo se llama "Kalahari." Pero I'll hafta get back to you on that, ya que no me atrevo a penetrar al baño pa' checar; el Steve is still in there, sort of huffin' and puffin' . . .

Hoy sí fui en un health walk, ¿eh? Pero abbreviated, por temor al COUGAR. I think I'm gonna switch to that name. Digo, en vez del genérico "mountain lion." Me encanta; it seems more rough 'n' tough, somehow. Also, me recuerda ese Walt Disney movie, no me acuerdo cómo se llama, pero it had a *most* dreadful, terrifying, cornered-cougar-snarling-and-lashing-out-at-young-boy moment, do you know which film I mean? (NB: When I e-mailed this croniquita to Santo-Amor, me dijo que ese film se llama *The Other Side of the Mountain.* ¡Gracias, bebé!)

First I went straight up that bifurcated drivewaylike colina, past the glass-walled, cubelike studio (la artista who lives in there, una tal Nilea, escultora, has already e-mailed me, pero I digress: more on her later, quizás) and up to the kind of vaguely menacing, cinderblock bunkerish ones. Llevaba los Chung Shi shoes, against my own pronouncements *and* better judgement (pues el balance no es exactamente mi strong suit, y este lugar tiene un terreno *bien* daunting, hilly, gravelly). Pero I figured, si iba a hacer sólo un short health hike, por lo del cougar, I'd better al menos wear las adrede unsteadying, wedge-soled health tackies, and super-challenge the nalgas, piernas, etc., ¿no?

I then walked back down, through the resident artist parking lot (LITTE EYE: todavía medio tripeo que *I'm* one of them, a resident artist), up that one-way road donde fuimos ayer (¿sólo ayer? Somehow it already seems like aeons ago that Pierre was here), pero en coche. Everything seemed to take *way* longer. Well, duh, a pie! That was when I saw that scatter of horsing-around teeny schoolkids on the lawns. Con un determined health-walk pace, I skirted the right side of the villa. Vi ese senderito leading up to that poet walk and the rock-hewn torture-stairs, and then I saw some more woodsy paths leading off to the right. Como Dante (or was it Petrarca? Oh, Bob Durling, petrarquista *non plus ultra* en Berkeley, I *wish* you could set me straight on this!), opté por la diestra.

Sentí que my pulse was racing. A light sheen of sweat had already come out, all over me, after only about ten minutes. ¡Coño! Decidí checar con el Dr. Scott on the Internido, en el Kaiser Permanente website, right after I got back to the studio (assuming I *made* it back, rather than making it into the fauces y garras de un wild beast), about time versus sudor. I mean: no *güey* could I keep up my normal health-walk pace for thirty-eight minutes as usual, con todos estos extreme ups and downs, y las strenuous, treacherous conditions. Gente, es friggin' *tenaz* por aquí, como diría mi gran pana, Juan Carlos "el colombiano" Galeano: pine needles a slick mat underfoot; moss and wild maidenhair ferns al ladito del sendero, just lurking there, pa' atrapar un tobillo; possible pumas en las copas de los redwoods y robles gigantescos.

I pushed on, I pushed myelf. Mientras caminaba, I made absurd, slight puffing and chuffing, catlike noises, como las Niñas. Aka mis gatas, Esmeralda y Alejandra. El trucho Steve Earle had advised me to "make noise," so I figured a feline-esque noise would be about the best. El corazón estaba *thump thump thump*. La verdad, estaba aterrada. This— just this, estos diez, quince minutos of dusty, foresty hills, only yardas away from "la civilización" (and what civilization, I mean come *on,* we're talking about a villa, for Chrissake!)—was *way* past my "comfort zone"! Why oh why has it always been so sort of fraught for me to interact like a normal person con la naturaleza (esto creo que lo heredé de mi papá, conste)? I mean, I *do* love it, the great outdoors, y la gente que sólo está getting to know me in the past few years siempre comenta mi fijación botánica, mi astonishing familiarity with international flora *and* fauna. Pero, sigh. I really should confess que (casi) siempre es mejor in theory, o al menos, como recuerdo.

Except for Australia. Por ejemplo, Magnetic Island, which literally *was* magnetic (el reloj del Paulie se detuvo misteriosa pero contundentemente en el ferry, on the way over from the mainland, from Townsville, y nunca más volvió a trabajar bien, la verdad). Esa isla era idyllic, blissful, gorgeous. Digo, en la vida real. In real time. My Robinson Crusoe day, explorando esa pequeña isla prácticamente de cabo a rabo, listening to the unfamiliar bird calls and the wind rustling the croton and massangeana fronds, sacando fotos de exotic flora y fauna. Pero OBvio, tenía la certeza de que practically the most frightening fauna posible eran los koalas—¡por favor! Or, OK, quizás esos crazy-eyed, shrieking, nocturnal curlews. Remember, Pierre? Remember, Paulie?

CRONICA INTERRUPTA:

OK. Dios me libre, el Steve ha arreglado lo de la ducha, pero remember el lock de arriba, the one he so-called fixed, which really wasn't? Pues ahora que él subió pa' vigilarme abrir y cerrar la puerta, well, it's fucking *working.* Trabaja, just like when you go to the mechanic and try to get your car to make the evil, annoying sound it's been doing for you prácticamente every time you start it up y no lo hace, you can't *get* it to happen, you know? Anygüey, like that.

So, I reckon I'll trot the laptop arriba el spiral staircase, al loft, al treehouse como lo llamo, plug it in, con todo y los speakers, and see if I can't join the twenty-first century. Heme aquí: con los iTunes implanted in there y todo (yeah, Santo-Amor, did you ever think you'd see *this* day? Maybe one day I'll even be burning a custom CD para ti, hey?

O mandándote shared archivos, aunque la verdad, ya que siempre se te está pegando one virus or another, mysterious computer meltdowns all over the show, capaz I'll just stay pure, ja ja, a file-sharer virgen). Hay que admitir que it's still a bit too much multitasking para mí, música *and* writing a la vez, out of the same machine. No me cuadra, really; I've never understood a la gente that can do both or more at once. Moving from document to document, different applications and programas, all over the show. Yo personalmente me pongo *muy* nerviosa that I'll hit some wrong button and it'll all explode, o me borro algo imprescindible with some little keystroke. O algo. Shit happens, ¿qué no?

Esta casita—working studio, le dicen—is teensy. Parece más bien huge from the outside, hasta ponderous, architect-designed y todo. Pero desde adentro, es como si estuviera en Manhattan, excepto que estoy en el forest. Y todo parece trabajar semi-rasquache, la verdad (el lock, la ducha, the medieval torture rack que pasa para cama). Pero I can't get over the glass wall, and the always-moving wall of green beyond. It *is* (muy de otra estirpe than Iguazú Falls, it's true) my own private *Green Mansions* all over again. Y just now el Steve told me, independent of my opinion, that *this* very one is the nicest studio. The nicest living space.

Hay que recalcar que me platicó un veritable chingo el vato, and for a nanosecond pensé wrily, uf, he's a *talker*. Pero then again, um . . . so can I be, bueno, al menos sometimes (OK, a lot), and so, I decided just to surrender. Decidí: What's my hurry? Me contó su life story, where he grew up (in the Valley, como yo), all the jobs he's done, de cuando conoció a John Wayne, when he worked in "the industry" y, claro, de sus destrezas outdoorsy. Y, just by the way, de su older daughter que habla perfecto español, learned in Argentina. You see? No hay coincidencias. Basically, se quedó like over an hour charle que charle, hasta que mi celular hizo un little beep, y thankfully, era un textual de Pierre. So, over 'n' out.

Si me quieren contactar, send me textuals (Qué ironía, ¿qué no? Hace seis meses I barely even had a clue what they were y ahora, desde que estoy en el Retrete, I've already been doing so many que Pierre, alarmado, va a tener que pedir un suplemento, renegotiate our phone contract con Verizon, me dijo). Or send me e-mails. Para variar: el cel service SUCKS here. La Cronopia Raz me platicó hoy que el Montalvo Arts Center está like in a vortex, como en una especie de bizarre dead zone. That when she drives right by here, en la Highway 9, *precisamente* en el turn for the Montalvo Arboretum, the phone goes dead. Just my luck. ¡Incomunicada! Pero maybe that's exactly what I need. Anygüey, gente, e-mail me, OK?

XI

South Coast Plaza Crónica

30 December 2006
Los Angeles

For Laura "Wiggue" Silverman, Pablo "Hugo" Zambrano,
and Tommy McGhee

Of course, se pueden imaginar the complete relief I feel after my
BUSTO scare. Haven't been able to "do" much of anything for a few
days, primero por la hideous ansiedad (o *anguhtia,* como dicen en Argentina) de la espera, de no saber, y ahora, in that bland, soft, floaty relief del después. So, to celebrate the fact of my non-imminent salida de
la vida, Pierre and I went to South Coast Plaza yesterday—antaño nuestro mall preferido. We hadn't been in a while, probably al menos un par
de años.

Anygüey, you know me, lo supersticiosa que soy: había prometido
que if I did not have cáncer del buhto I would STOP de una puta vez
putting myself down phobically about los looks, dizque weight issues

(conste, la B-2 dice que tengo un light case of body dysmorphia, y bueno, she's a nutritionist, she should know, ¿no?), y otros "superficial" topix like that.

Pero unfortunately, less than twenty-four hours after my latest solemn vows to be ABOVE IT ALL, in the ritzy (I mean: YSL, Donna Karan, Louis Vuitton, Gucci, Armani, Ron Herman, D&G, ad nauseum) shop windows I caught a glimpse of myself bajo las despiadadas luces fluorescentes del mall and harshly judged myself as *wanting*. Al mirarme con ojo crítico (what other kind do I have, la neta?), I looked haggard. ¡Mi peor fobia! Definitely *not* hip. Mis cabellos, my dizque crowning gloria de rulos castaños, de repente se miraban straggly, almost dweedly. Peor, of *no* color found in la naturaleza. What *is* that orange? OMG: hay que poner a Raimundo Riojas, mi peluquero, on speed-dial. Joder. Para colmo me sentía, de repente, horribly underdressed compared to the multitudes of teensy, coltish O.C. Asian or (equally teensy pero también) pneumatically busto- and lip-inflated, blow-arriba dolls, las blonde, suburban socialite housewives who frequent South Coast Plaza.

I cursed my need for gafas (even if Prada), really, hay que admitirlo, pretty much 24/7 now. Porque me parece que me ofuscan mi "mejor" feature: los ojos. Bueno, at least they *used* to be. Digo, mi best feature. I also cursed my indigo velvet DKNY pants, inherited from Tommy McGhee (pareja de Raphy), which I always thought made me look so louche, digámoslo, tan directamente *hot* in Argentina. Pero ayer, in those South Coast Plaza store vitrinas, I saw them for what they are: baggy in the nalga and then falling unfashionably straight, casi PEG-legged. Uf! ¡Chale! Definitivamente *out* y poco flattering.

What was I thinking? Los había estado guardando. I'd hung on, clung on to them cual náufrago a life raft durante los dos años of my discontent, of my metabolic slowdown and concomitante blimpificación, debida a las fucking beta-blockers (único grave error del otherwise superlative Dr. Scott: recetarme esas malditas pahtishas). I had been waiting, biding my time till I could once again pull them on in all their baggy glory y sentirme sylphlike, sexy. Like I did in the southern hemisphere.

Y ahora, I can. Que health diet, yoga, cero martini lunches y sobre todo, sobre todo, mis health walks, three, four, a veces *five* times a week. Five kilometers de speed walking y hasta running, in little bursts (a *esto* lo llaman interval training, me lo dijo mi advisee la Elaine McGlaughlin, experta runner: debo recordarlo) until my lungs swell to bursting and words combine and rub and jostle, exploding in my brain, sentidos y poros abiertos to the sight of a sudden, whirling hawk, a startling whiff of damp skunk grass, or to pods and buds everywhere abriéndose en la too-early primavera last winter y ahora, a las curled brown leaves scuttling underfoot en la extrema sequedad de lo que se llama invierno aquí en SoCal these days.

I can pull those velvet trousers on again. They slip on with ease, not digging or clinging anywhere. You'd think I'd be satisfied. Sobre la luna, de hecho, ¿no? Pero you know me: me miré en esos fucking funhouse mirror shop windows and just thought: ugh. Me veo como alguna especie de weird Tyrolian troll.

Anygüey, another bajón: *todos* los sit-down restaurants have departed South Coast Plaza. Años ha desapareció the Magic Pan, the San Francisco–based creperie that for years soothingly me recordaba los student days, en la UC–Irvine, cuando iba a South Coast Plaza con mi amiga Elsa Saucedo, just to ogle las para nosotras then untouchable (OK, except for Judy's! También long-gone . . .) vitrinas and lunch on creamed-spinach crepes. Ayer vinimos a descubrir que Troquet has also closed. Just recently. ¡Coño! I mean, *that* restaurant was an institution.

Pierre teorizó que maybe it was giving people los willies—giving off vaguely rasquache vibes, you know—la idea de frecuentar un ritzy, sit-down restó in a mall. Anygüey, Troquet had been there for years, for *aeons* sin que la gente tuviera esa asociación. Pero a mí se me hace que the mall's days are numbered, ¿qué no? Quiero decir malls in general. Como institución. Los *shopping,* como les dicen en Argentina. Y este thought me pone bien melancólica, somehow.

Bueno, el highlight de ayer was going to the special, teensy perfume salon dentro del Nordstrom. As per usual, nadie podía ayudarme a rastrear mi holy grail, el *7e Sens* de Sonia Rykiel. It did not even feature en ese big, huge perfume book que tienen los experts, donde te dicen what family a scent belongs to, and even sometimes hasta los ingredientes, even of some long-ago disappeared scents. Pero in compensation, Pierre me compró Maitre Parfumeur et Gantier's *Secrete Datura.* Oh my God, it comes in a humongous bottle, y es unspeakably expensive. Había recibido una muestra cuando Pierre encargó un Lafco candle de Aedes de Venustas en N.Y.C. (recomendado por mi hermana Wiggue, OB-vio), and I'd become sort of obsessed with its slightly sinister, swooningly floral, heavy fragrance.

Bueno, una tal Lynda Lieb, la "certified fragrance specialist" de Nordstrom (aunque, como recalcó Pierre, how *could* she call herself that y no hablar palabra de French?), me contó que *datura* is the trumpet flower. Yes, that big ol' huge flower que le digo la scrotal flower, esa planta que tienen mi hairdresser Raimundo and his wife la Tere en su yarda: it droops down, enormous and phallic, y despide un creamy, dreamy, heavy, utterly torrid scent, a toda hora, pero *especially* de noche, all throughout the year. La Lynda me dijo que the datura has a long mythology, que hasta es venenosa y se considera muy peligrosa y magic in some circles. *Natuurlik,* después de ese sales pitch, I immediately snapped it up.

Pero casi más interesante: mientras le platicaba de los perfumes que más me enloquecen (you know, *Diva* by Ungaro, Norma Kamali's *Body Incense*—a pure shot of iglesia católica to the venas—Guerlain's *Vetiver,* YSL's *Kouros,* etc.), she said she just *knew* I'd love Miller Harris's *Feuilles de Tabac,* del cual ella sólo tenía una teensy muestra, which she couldn't let me have porque she *herself* planned to wear it on New Year's Eve. Can you believe la mejilla? Pero me roció, and she said: Now just wait, walk around, and in about an hour, then you'll see.

Oh my God, so true! Al principio, me cayó sort of masculine, and maybe even a bit generic. A little bit *Givenchy Gentleman* (still swoony in an Armin Schwegler kind of way, después de todos estos años), a little bit *Polo.* Quizás como *Halston Z-14 for Men,* de los late '70s. Pero then it warmed and bloomed on my wrist. Olía a tabaco, pero también a verde. Cero powder. It was an insistent, subtle, bisexual, bewitching scent. I could not get enough of my wrist. Y duró horas. Me lo había hecho spray la Lynda, from her precious vial, como a la una de la tarde. A las siete, al salir del cine (we'd gone to see *Pan's Labyrinth,* Guillermo del Toro's new one, and it was fantastic, me regresó a mi early childhood en España—pero esa es otra), I could still faintly smell it. I *must* acquire it.

Y bueno. What about my extremadamente bajoneantes image issues de asher?

Pos, bien Scarlet O'Hara–like (EYE: ella es otra famosa Aries): tomorrow es otro día, ¿qué no? So hoy por hoy, I will just push those blue velvet trousers to the back of the placard (I *must* save them forever, ya saben lo sappy que soy; me recuerdan—me hacen acordar—a Tommy, and of my year en el sur del Sur), apply some firming eye gel y encarar— hasta con gratitud—este almost año nuevo.

XII

I Want the Wrapper Crónica

29 octubre 2007
Somewhere en el Inland Empire
de Califas

For Paul Saint-Amour

When I told you, a few weeks ago, aboard ese slow-as-lodo SEPTA commuter train que nos regresaba de Philly a un rainy, muggy y *mega*-stuck-up Princeton, tu nuevo "hometown," que me sacaba de onda entrar a Rhino Records en el Village de Claremont, to browse through music, por la posible preponderancia de über-hip apenitas post-teens, te me reíste. You told me que la única gente que todavía, a estas alturas, *sigue* buying albums (como se les dice, metafórica, ¿nostálgicamente? a los CD) are middle-age geeks anyway. In other words, que no me sintiera inhibited about going in there.

LITTLE EYE: conozco el mundo de tu iPod shuffle, de los randomly generated playlists. Uno para cada mood, for *any* mood. I know all about los downloads, el "Boob" (You) Tube, MySpace, or Facebook (el

88

CaraBobo, I call it), o como corno se llame. And EYE: lately hasta textualizo—o mando SMS's, como les dicen en South Africa, en España—along with the best of 'em (lo cual todavía *no* te ha atrapado a ti, which shocks the infierno outta me!). Y no es que me sienta threatened by, no siento miedo ni inferioridad hacia, los cyber-savvy teens y veinte-algos. Son mis estudiantes. Son mis amigos. Hell, they're some of my biggest fans. ¿Irónico?

Por ejemplo, te juro que en Bryn Mawr el otro día, after my reading, this adorable, punky, Goth-looking, mega-pierced, dykey coed (from whom I'd timidly asked directions a la librería, earlier in the day) me dijo, "Can I just *tell* you how dope and fly you are?" Pero anygüey, my point is: que se queden con los teensy, pearlescent, white-earbud-sprouting winkie wankies. Blocking out the birdcalls, blotting out los menacing—or tempting—city-street sounds: bocinas, babies, gente hablando (si bien casi siempre en su cel phone . . .).

Yo todavía quiero *todo* y el wrapper too, baby. Esta actitud te parecerá shockingly pre-PoMo, pero ni modo. Y sé que esto me aproxima, perilously, a la recontra outmoded, demoted reverence for . . . authorial or artistic *intention*. And other Modernist shit like that (the horror, the horror). Pero me arriesgo, I'll press home: I want the whole package; quiero hojear el little booklet, para poder sonreirme, semi-smugly, al descubrir que Ben Harper dedica su latest CD a mis lares (sus ex-lares!): el Inland Empire. Quiero verlo, tocarlo todo, just as it was lovingly assembled. O al menos conceived, ¿no?

What would I do without contemplating Bruce's face as he belts out the first notes of (the admittedly tinny and overproduced) "Radio Nowhere": still chiseled, committed, melancholy, desafiante. Quiero checar el look también, I admit it freely, de su band. See how they've held up over the years (coño, casi treinta, *can* it be?). El Nils Lofgren played the most smoldering solo guitar licks of just about anyone cuando yo estaba en la high school. Y en los conciertos, he used to lance himself, su elfin, compact, sexy cuerpo went airborne, te lo juro, haciendo unbelievable somersaults, all across the stage. Pero hace años que ese su blustery bad-boy swagger está domesticado; su incendiary guitarra a veces todavía es la principal, it's true (como en "Tunnel of Love," por ejemplo), pero he's mos def a backup vocalist now. One of the boys in the band.

Y la Patti Scialfa, she of that brief blaze of "Rumble Doll" gloria (consigned right away a los remainder bins, pero, ¿quién no? Who the hell isn't?). Oyeme Patti, did you capitulate, mute the ferocity of your longing, contenta en la entrega entre tus muslos? Being Bruce's mujer, la musa de Bruce, making love to el Jefe, bearing his three kids? Taming, shaping esa tu antaño soaring, wild voice para armonizar con Bruce.

¿Y yo? ¿Me entregué? Did I give (myself) up, give in? Dando a luz a Etienne, al Juvenil. My crowning moment? Y todo lo que ha seguido a ese momento (which sure as hell dethroned my Ph.D. exam—tomado sólo cuatro días antes de dar a luz—as the most intense, physically challenging experiencia de mi vida): what does it all mean? ¿Qué pacto sellé, cuáles renuncias? Haber aceptado—no, having *stuck* with, más bien, como manso buey—el trabajo de docente en un liberal arts college. Predictable. Health insurance (OK, es HMO, but still . . .), 401(k). Y la chamba itself: cada vez menos edgy, más burocratizada.

Paul, I don't really have answers for these questions. Ni, for that matter, a casi ninguna otra. Pero eso sí: as I head down the Thompson Creek trail esta mañana, iPodless, tuning in, instead, to a chirpy sky just beginning to clear of post-wildfire smoke and ash—por apocalíptico que parezca, just the "typical" Califas fall conflagration—I *do* know one thing for sure. Si el Bruce was born to run, yo nací para escribir.

P.S. OB-vio, this was written *justo* antes de que los mercados, los 401(k)s, los banks, los mortgages . . . well, you all know—and share—the story, ¿qué no?

XIII

Mini Geography Lesson Crónica

6 marzo 2006
Claramonte, Califas

Para mis estudiantes, with whom I've discussed this y tantos otros temas, and
for HHG, my gunsteling delwer

I like things messy. A tangle of skin, minds, heat, soul, heart. Entre la curiosidad y el miedo—las dos orientaciones fundamentales hacia la vida, según Cortázar—la primera siempre (me) gana. Always has. And always will, esperemos (singed whiskers no obstante).

I like things real, también. Por eso me choca toda esta fundamental duplicidad, the glaring hypocrisy de delimitar todo lo que es y no es (post-AIDS? post-Clinton?) "el sexo." All that back-to-basics, essentialist parceling out of desire, de lo propio. Returning to or staying within ese limitado paradigma binario. Making it—grado superlativo, ¿no?—*all* about insertion. Penetration. Completion. Cuando las partes "correctas" se encuentran, se incrustan, se juntan.

Si "el sexo" puede ser . . . *everything,* sin estos limits. Estos safety nets. Todo. O hasta (casi) nada. An infinitely small gesture, hasta algo (casi) irreconocible. Walk out on that cuerda floja. Sólo depende de cómo estemos sintonizados, ¿no?

La vida, I mean, el sexo, lo erótico, is not—bueno, *should* not (only) be—all about true blue, I got you, you got me (coño, sounds like Sonny 'n' Cher, pero they were cool, *then*), delimitar la parcela de pasión correcta, (self) control.

El corazón humano es un terreno extraño, uncertain. En las alquímicas, geniales manos de Sor Juana Inés de la Cruz, the heart melts, liquifies; it manifests, hacia el final de ese lapidary *ars amandi*—her famous sonnet—en forma de lágrimas, objective correlative of her love, ante la mirada del amor celoso y cauteloso.

A veces el corazón es un baldío. Lunar landscape. Otras veces un pantano. Spongey. Drawing you in, down. Con todo y sus tembladerales. Quicksand. No hay topografía que más me hechice. The allure, precisamente, reside en lo unpredictable.

Ante la primera geografía, I feel like a miner. OJO: esto no es (sólo) metáfora. Yo sé de lo que hablo. I lived on a mine once. Con Howard. Allá en Cullinan, South Africa. The Premier Diamond Mine. Cerca de Pretoria. Tener que tantear el terreno, probing that harsh, forbidding surface. Aprender la diferencia entre la dinamita and the smallest, most precise chisel. Working at even just the insinuation of a flaw. Fomentando la ruptura, la grieta. Para que la superficie se fisure, se raje, revealing, finalmente, the treasure.

Esta primera topografía exige paciencia. Not my forte. ¿Será por eso, maybe, que me encuentro tantas veces amidst these arid rockeries, *chip chip chipping* away con mi pickaxe—mi corazón, mi escritura: my heartfelt words—intentando descubrir la veta sin provocar la avalancha que lo arrasa todo?

El segundo terreno me es menos incógnito. I was born along a similar latitude. Still, ante un pantano desconocido, I tremble, jadeo levemente. Me siento desorientada, upside down, en alerta. Waiting for the anaconda's strike, the camouflaged enemy's hushed footfall.

Estas operaciones telúricas me cuestan, me iluminan, me estrujan. Pero acepto estar ante estas *dos* geografías: one moment skimming over, probing la superficie de la luna, remote, austere, forbidding; the next foraying through green mansions, inviting, si peligrosas. Andale, bid me welcome.

XIV

Arañita Cobriza Crónica

30 noviembre 2007
Inland Imperio de Califas

For Wim "OomBie" Lindeque

Te pedí que eligieras un lugar en el mundo, un lugar ideal para transportarme, transportarnos. Si fuera un mundo ilimitado, I'd have asked you to just drive, straight through to Joshua Tree. Amo el desierto; aprendí el año pasado que you do too. Pero como el mundo siempre quiere invadir nuestros secret gardens, con sus clausuras, we had a time limit, after all.

With you, time always flows y se detiene a la vez. It brushes over me, casi imperceptible, cual ala de gran ave protector; it whirls around me, vórtice, vertiginous yet transfixing.

Me dijiste que you wouldn't know where to take me, aquí en Califas. Pero it was you who said, finalmente: How about el Jardín Botánico? You *did* know where to take me, after all. Exactly. (How did you know?)

Caminamos. I walked a half step ahead of you, para que me apreciaras los copper-colored ultrasuede Max Studio pantalones, the length of my stride en los Ríos of Mercedes authentic cowboy boots from Santa Fe. Sentimos el olor de las native-to-the-southwest plantas: la salvia. Always my homecoming scent. The soft dryness of mimosa-powdery dust bajo los eucaliptos y pinos. En vano buscamos las palmeras. You had promised to take me to them. Pero, ¿las buscamos, realmente? ¿Qué buscamos? I think maybe we were just looking to get lost. Como esa Chet Baker song.

En un momento bien Hansel y Gretel, vi un banquito bajo la sombra de unos pinos gigantescos. This place felt different, mucho más northern Califas. It was at the end of a gravel path, sheltered, secreto. El banco era weird. It was sweetly curved; it cupped our nalgas, enveloped us, nos acurrucó. Hablamos de Sudáfrica. De la infancia y nuestros libros, sueños, miedos. Estuvimos en silencio and it was cloudlike. Caían las hojas, soft as feathers en la leve brisa invernal. Woodpeckers and doves made their sounds, industriosos o sosegantes. Faraway, una sierra. *Zzz, zzz* . . . Strangely, no nos invadía. Llegó a sentirse como una mantra.

Sentí intensamente tu presencia, como hace años, uncannily, the pressure of your body on mine. Macizo. Cálido. Comforting. Sentí el pulso en mi garganta. Me sentí a la vez flotante y anclada. This is how I feel with you: lost (and found) in space.

Con los brazos entrelazados, my bare forearm resting ever so lightly across your thighs as we talked, me observaste de repente una minúscula araña en la mano. You *know* about me and bears. ¿Te había contado alguna vez de las arañas? They don't frighten me, not at all; me intrigan.

El tiempo se detuvo entonces, en un surprising, hypnotic lull. Esa teensy copper-red spider, like a pinprick of blood, traced her path, allegorically, over our outstretched, yearning, interlaced fingers, palms, wrists. Nuestros dedos seguían, soñolientos, dreamily, su caminito.

Luego caminamos de nuevo, overtaken by hunger, conscientes del tiempo. Pausamos, close to a rough-hewn gate, looking into some kind of ranch, viendo pasar vehículos que yo te recordaba eran como los safari guide jeeps, for game spotting. Quise imaginar que we were back in Africa. Como en el Mabula Game Lodge, con Manja y Teenie, *onthou jy?* Como fingimos que we were on our luna de miel?

We stood there for a while y era romántico, Wild West–ish, "Deadwood"-y, o bien Heath Ledger–like (Q.E.P.D.). That dusty, quintessentially North American panorama, el viento fresco en la piel; hacía casi frío a pesar del sol. Leaning on that fence y mirándonos de reojo. Reminiscing. Recordando. Out of the corner of my eye mirarte as you lounged, de repente graceful, felino, sólo un teensy flash of panza entre tus brand-new Levis y striped polo shirt.

Hubo esto y hubo mucho más. Hubo la parte por ejemplo, still huddled together, en ese banco, cuando te comencé a contar, haltingly, con los ojos cerrados a veces para mejor recordar (para esquivar sólo un poco— I confess—el dizzyingly too-close escrutinio de tu gaze) fragmentos de un sueño.

Pero contarte ese y tantos otros sueños es otro encuentro, another crónica. A desert drive, ¿quizás? For now, me quedo con esa arañita.

XV

Westside Desilusión Crónica

12 May 2006
Los Angeles

For Laura "Wiggue" Chávez Silverman and
for Elaine S. "Miss Elaine" Brooks, en su cumpleaños

Pierre and I drove all the way out to UCLA last night, for a much-anticipated concierto de Richard Thompson. Tú y yo lo vimos en Berkeley, aeons ago, con Bonnie Raitt, remember? A couple of years after I'd returned from South Africa, y estaba en el programa doctoral en UC–Davis. Ni pihta who *you* were with esa noche: Eddie? Rupert Pelota-Verde? All I know is we had Indian food, y ese concierto was smokin'. Anygüey, el R.T. is one of the best guitarristas in the world.

Bueno, first off, nos tomó *más* de dos horas y media to get there. Según Mapquest, it *should* take fifty-two minutes, pero eso es en el Internido, un hypermundo, mos def not la real-life cuenca de L.A. durante la dizque rush hour. "So-called" porque la hora pico is pretty much 24/7 these days. The 10W through downtown was a pesadilla; luego the 405N (dad's ex-commute, de UCLA back home, to the Valley) hasta la Sunset was at a standstill. Te lo juro. Literally, nos tomó más de media hora to go, like, *three* exits!!!

Por toda esa jodienda del traffic, tuvimos un *extremely* rushed dinner en Westwood con Licha (aka Alicia Gaspar de Alba, la escritora chicana, remember? La conociste en mi casa). She teaches at UCLA. Nos llevó a Eurochow, un super-trendy restó en un enorme edificio, used to be a bank. White, todo todo blanco, with little glowing lucite cubes en las mesas, que eran de cristal. Muchos comensales recontra *fashion* (como quien dice en Buenos Aires, means, you know, hip, cool) wearing large, Prada-esque heavy black gafas. La comida fue riquísima. It was good to see la Licha, aun en una comida tan rushed. We hadn't seen her in months. Ella sigue comiendo Atkins-style, which I love, especialmente in theory. I don't give in all that often, pero it really is what my O-pos blood type craves: red meat and lots of it (sigh, *only* in Argentina). Pero la Licha ha dejado de tomar, so I felt kind of bad, pidiendo un martini. Pero pos ni modo.

El concierto, desafortunadamente, proved to be el gran guitar god del Richard Thompson (resident en Pacific Palisades for the last thirteen years . . . how *can* he remain so quintessentially, even resolutely británico? Hmmmmm. Quizás sea, precisamente, porque *no* vive en el UK), playing a millennium's worth of popular music, acompañado de una BIZARRE, twirling rubia. Una overwrought chanteuse, wannabe Stevie Nicks, llamada Judith. Ay, you know. Una de esas gauze-swathed, faux-Druids. Como compensación, la drummer se parecía a nuestra faux-prima, la Lee Weiss; era fenomenal baterista y bastante good singer too. Mucho mejor que la wannabe Stevie.

Well, entre su choice of songs (which included covers of Cole Porter, Nat King Cole, algunas medieval troubadourlike songs—which were, la verdad, lo mejor del concierto—the Beatles, Ben Folds, and ugh, la Britney Assegai's "Oops, lo hice de nuevo") y esa atroz acompañante la tal Judith (a quien el Richard permitió que cantara on her own *far* too many times), the whole thing sucked. Pero *bigtime*. You *know* I disen-JOY that show-tune, cabaret effect.

Hasta en los encores, although el público le rogó, fíjate que el Richard did not play one *single* song of his own. Pos chale to *that*. Hasta triple-chale, as my friend Alicia Garza would say. What a letdown. So anygüey, casi cinco horas (total) de freeway driving for that bazofia. Sigh.

Toda esta discouraging experiencia pretty much tronchó una fantasía I've been entertaining lately, about somehow quizás getting a gig at USC or UCLA pa' mis declining years (kind of *reversing* dad's trayec-toria: a slightly creepy prospect, incluso en el mejor de los mundos po-sibles, ¿no?). Estuve pensando: si sólo pudiera . . . qué sé sho, land some combo deal, like in Spanish and creative writing; OB-vio, sin los heavy committee or teaching duties, capaz pudiera, algún día, hacerse reali-dad my long-cherished dream: una casa en el Westside.

Pero, sigh. We could *never* afford Westwood, ni siquiera any other of the even *semi*-close-to-UCLA barrios en un sueldo cacadémico, no matter how "good." Licha, por ejemplo, acaba de comprarse un minúhculo two-bedroom condo allá por Westchester, for around a half a million, me parece. No lejos de la casa que se compraron ella y la "Shirlie," like five years ago. Pero anygüey, ese little condo le costó al-most what they paid for that humongous house! So, pa' qué toda la mu-danza, just to be en otro condo, possibly hasta smaller than where we are now? Capaz hasta en una casita *bien* rasquache, fixer-upper and teeny tiny. Sin duda, for the privilegio de vivir en el über-hip Westside, tendríamos que cough up, mínimo, dos veces what the Claramonte pad is now worth. "Worth" entre comishas, ¿no? Es todo relativo.

So, entre el obscene unaffordability y el daunting prospect de tener que wade through all those desperate metallic beetles, bobbing and weaving entre ese phalanx de inured road guerreros, every day, pa' hacer el com-mute to Pomona College, pues como que it doesn't look like I'll *ever* get out of el Evil Imperio. Ya sabes cuánto me saca de onda conducir. Not talking about los road trips! Eso es otra cosa. Eso es lo mío. Pero I mean

I'd hate to *have* to drive, hacer el condemned commute, para hacer mi vida cotidiana.

So, parece que I'll just have to keep on dreaming. And driving . . . pero LITTLE EYE: *sólo* para ir a los earth-shatteringly kick-nalga EVEN-TOS CULTURALES, como este Richard Thompson concierto, ¿no?

There Was Blood Diptych

XVI

Unos Cuantos Piquetitos
Crónica

8 January 2008
Somewhere en el Evil, oops, <u>Inland</u> Imperio de Califas

For Laura "Lauris" Gutiérrez, Elaine S. Brooks, Raphael Kadushin y Florence "la Flor" Moorhead-Rosenberg, Tauruses all, con amor y sangre

For Frida Kahlo, in memoriam

Well, mi colega y amigo el José C-2 accompanied me to the hospie yesterday for a biopsy. It was *extremely* unpleasant, to say the least, and, as could be predicted, my BP was off the radar, que digamos Richter (more el upper que el lower numerito, pero I forget which way is more dire, lo cual me hace stress out even more, OB-vio . . .) en los momentos just before the "procedure." I am trying not to be *too* alarmed about that, since the arribas and abajos of my BP are *intimately* related to my emo state, and I've been faithfully using my new RESPeRATE machine, que te hace una especie de biofeedback pa' aletargarte la breathing. Plus,

he seguido con el estúpido sécate-*toditita* diuretic, los health walks, y
bla bla (ay, todo *tan* boring).

Anygüey, I won't go into detalle about el procedimiento mismo: it was
unnerving, demoralizing, and mega-estresante, even bajo los efectos del
Xanax *and* local lidocane (the installation of which was maybe even casi
casi lo PEOR). Por suerte, the pathologist who performed the stereotactic NEEDLE biopsy era un puertorriqueño who appreciated the
bizarre humor I was somehow able to muster cuando, mientras yacía,
boca abajo, en ese heartlessly cold metal table (images of la parrisha—
como le decían al torture table que usaban durante la dictadura en
Argentina—kept popping into my admittedly paranoid and hyperbolic
imaginación), le pregunté, apropos of a teensy titanium CLIP (?) they
inserted into my buhto—AND LEFT THERE—supuestamente at the
precise site of the microcalcificaciones, if I was now *officially* some sort
of sci-fi alien. El tipo, cool as a pepino, hasta me hizo un little quip
patrás: "Why, are you an *unofficial* alien now?"

Actually, it is the thought of having that tiny "clip" inside me, in such
an intimate locus of my geografía interior, that I find most unsettling
and yet (bueno, you *know* how genuinely strange I am) . . . also somehow hechizante. En la X-ray que me mostró el médico, it looks a bit
like a tiny (we're talking about the size of a pen point) antenna, or a
blue ribbon (as the Chicana nurse, Melissa, cheerfully prompted me
to appreciate). To me, it looks most like the glyph for the astrological
sign Taurus, el signo de varios de mis máximos carnales. And so, I will
hold on to the idea of this astro-semaphore. Me reconforta, de alguna
manera, la idea de llevarlos a Uds. tan close to my too-excitable heart,
entangled con mis entrañas . . . and in imminent danger (aunque el pa-
tólogo assured me this would not happen!) of setting off los metal de-
tectors en los aeropuertos.

Can you imagine? First my twenty-four South African bracelets—que
eventualmente tuve que dejar de llevar, por el tema del beefed-up secur-
ity en los aeropuertos, post 9/11, después de más de veinte años, so
much *clink clink* and weight on that left side; I even gave birth in them,

¡coño!—and now un Taurean titanium clip, marking off the site of *former* microcalcificaciones busteriles.

Mientras me hacían la jodida biopsia, the nurse had to call in una über-enfermera, porque aparentemente, there was a blood vessel too close to the site of the little chips de calcio, and they had to do this *most* uncomfy busto-manipulating operación to get it (la vesícula) out of the way.

Bueno, al regresar a casa entré al cobalt blue–painted guest bath, abajo. I took in the fantastic, little-girl-lost Camille Rose García prints, the beautiful caldera-colored, glass-mosaic-tiled counter, the gorgeously Goth, black, drippy-looking wrought iron light fixture, worthy of *The Addams Family,* installed by Pierre en las últimas refacciones del 2006. I took off my ancient (according to fashion's ever-fickle seasons) black Prada ski jacket (second-hand regalo de mi hermana Laura, aka la Wiggue, before I went to Buenos Aires for the first time, en el '99—y creo que estaba past-season even *then*!). In that penumbral, Alice in Wonderland a lo Chicana luz, I saw three uncannily beautiful pero *definitely* crimson spots flowering on my chest, left side. I wriggled out of the left side of my gray American Apparel raglan-sleeved, tissue-weight cotton sweatshirt, cupped my breast instinctively, and my hand came away filled with blood.

Como en una película de horror, like in *Carrie,* la sangre saturaba el petite round ice pack que las enfermeras me habían insertado en el sexy, sort of dominatrix, black lace Olga balconette bra (my good-luck corpiño). Todavía pathetically clutching my breast, con la bahtante menos eficaz diestra, I stripped off the top, y el bra; los tiré al sink con ese crimson ice pack, les eché agua fría encima and watched it bloom scarlet. Just like ese Easter egg dye que nos preparaba mamá, musité. Paas, I remembered. El espejo me devolvió una imagen espectral, pero oddly placid. Blood covered the left side of my torso. How could *so* much blood emerge from a tiny nick, pensé, y luego, immediately, pensé en el famoso cuadro de Frida Kahlo, "Unos cuantos piquetitos." Can you imagine? Typical me: there I am, dripping, pulsing, coursing sangre, pensando en la moda, en películas, en paintings.

I unzipped my gray-green Levi pinwale stretch cords; I was intensely conscious I would drip blood all over the floor; me preocupaban las Niñas, Esmeralda y Alejandra, que ya maullaban, worried (bueno, OK, also hungry, a decir verdad . . .). I suddenly remembered about pressure. Aplicar presión. I held my breast more insistently, con la right hand, pero somehow I couldn't believe that only *that* would staunch the flow. Llamé a Pierre al trabajo, porque él conoce un chingo de first aid, pero to my horror, he was barely even conscious himself, having been stricken con un fast-moving stomach flu. Apenitas tenía la fuerza, as it turned out, to drive himself home.

Para cuando llegó, I'd already spoken to the enfermera, y al mere mere Puerto Rican pathologist, quien me dijo que (*natuurlik*) lo que me pasó was "unusual," pero que there can always be some little artery or vesícula "in the way," invisible. A fount of unexpected blood. He told me, bien matter of fact, que hasta en el peor de los casos (cutting "a major artery," dijo, creo), if you apply pressure "for about an hour," it will stop.

Bueno, gente, apreté like there was no mañana; I set the little red, retro timer en la blood-red, PoMo, retro cocina, and pressed veinte minutos, como si fuera uno de los trials de Hércules.

It stopped.

By the time it stopped, though, había blood spatters on the made-in-Argentina (it's true, el downstairs floor tile hasta se shama "Pampa"), faux-Spanish—or faux-Mexican—Saltillo tile; blood had soaked through the rolled-up paper towel I was clutching; it caked my hand, la axila, streaked my torso y hasta trickled down into my chonies. El full-length espejo en el living room, donde generalmente chequeo mi *look* antes de salir al mundo, me devolvió una imagen espeluznante. Ghoulish y compellingly erotic a la vez.

OK, OK, sha sé. Leave it to *me*.

Y bueno, it's Kaiser Permanente. It's an HMO mundo we inhabit (digo, those of us even lucky enough to *have* health care coverage), so I won't know anything for up to ten days, can you believe it? Y eso que sólo me van a llamar para hacer una cita for me to *return,* again, to that rasquache Kaiser Permanente hospital in the heart of the Evil, que digamos Inland Empire, en Fontana, Califas, para darme los resultados *in person.* Me dijeron: Whether the news is good or bad, they *have* to give it to you in person. Es la ley.

So now, a esperar. *Tic tac tic tac.* Um, *not* something my Grand Trine in fuego personality excels at, pero you already know that. Y . . . qué remedio, ¿no?

So, les escribo esto, my darling Tauruses, seeking comfort, seeking . . . que sé sho, connection. Sigh. As usual. My words looking for your words, wishing it were your eyes, your faces I could see, talking, reassuring, laughing with me. Pero for now, heme aquí, a la espera. All she wrote.

XVII

Momentos Hemorrágicos
Crónica

10 enero 2008 / 3 junio 2008
Claremont and Saratoga, Califas

For Howard H. Geach, met liefde en bloed,
and for Wim Lindeque and Joanna Martine Woolfolk

A June A. Chávez Silverman y
Etienne L. J. Kapp, in memoriam

$\mathcal{I}$ must be what they call a bleeder (uf, suena a oscuro insulto británico, ¿no?). I mean, I guess I *literally* am (ay, qué drama queen). Especially después de esto último: cuando el teensy agujero diagnóstico (por el cual me habían insertado un chip, I mean, un *clip* de titanium, para marcar el lugar de la herida and that Chris Sadiq, mi masajista, llama el "bionic chip") spouted blood. Luckily, a sólo dos días de esa catastrófica y sangrienta stereotactic biopsy—por la bondad del Dr. Scott and his willingness to flout o que digamos get a jump on the molasses-slow not to mention impersonal HMO system, transmitting the negative results de la biopsia en un e-mail—that baroquely problematic biopsy site ya no era, at least, un lugar de anguhtia. It itched, ached, and was turning black 'n' blue like a motherfucker—pero these were all quite acceptable efectos secundarios (*pace* Ani Shua: ¿Te acordás cuando traduje, outloud, en tu ponencia en Pomona, "secondary effects" for side efects? Completely sin querer! Oh my God, what an egger!), considerando la alternativa.

Pero *why* did I tell Melissa, la nurse que me atendía durante la biopsy, that I don't have a bleeding problem? I've always bruised rather dramatically, y ahora que me pongo a pensar un poco, about blood, habría que recordar esa vez a los nueve años. Before they could even *begin* orthodonture, por mi supposedly too-teensy palate me tuvieron que extirpar ten teeth. Simón, sé lo que digo. *Ten*! I know it sounds barbaric, impossible, pero es la verdad. OK, OK, eran four permanent teeth and six baby teeth, pero still. Ahora, lo que nunca me he podido explicar is why I not only agreed to it but I actually begged and wheedled and badgered, insistiendo en quedarme overnight en el hospital. Dumb, ¿o qué?

No era como ahora, que los niños hacen sleepovers cada dos por tres. A los nueve, I hadn't spent that many nights away from home. Bueno, on the rare occasion me quedaba en lo de mi vecina and best friend, la Maureen Hurley. Pero that was right next door. Y hubo también esa semana de Camp Fire Girls camp, que aborrecí. Yo era un poquito sissy (bueno, *very*), even at the best of times. Creo que I cried every single day, y eso que estaba también mi hermana Sarita. But she was still a Bluebird y hangueaba con sus propias homies. I hate hate *hated* it. Todo ese faux-outdoorsy shit. Esos beads we had to earn, como si fueran wampum, a certain number, shape, and color según la dificultad de la hazaña pseudo-indígena. Ese cuero trucho (antes de que fuera bautizado ultrasuede . . . hmmm, ¿no fue el designer Halston que lo llamó así?) we had to sew and thread the beads on. Yuck. Triple-chale, como dice mi amiga la Alicia Garza.

Y para peor, el hairdresser de mamá, el Buko, un encantador hindú feliz she used to go to, en Bullocks Wilshire, me había cortado los lunguísimos cabellos just the week before. Te lo juro. I went in with Mom, pa' su haircut, y el vato me pregunta: What do you want *all* that hair for?

Como no le pude contestar, me lo cortó. Just like that! Por poco me rapó. Hair down to my waist, o casi, y el tipo me da un fucking pixie sólo porque de pura pendeja I couldn't tell him why I was attached to my hair. Can you believe that? One of the worst hair moments de mi vida.

So anygüey, además de las outdoorsy indignities perpetrated on me, I kept a hideous, reversible floral cotton cap *glued* on my head the entire week en ese Camp Fire Girls camp, para tapar el odioso pixie cut. You can see me en fotos de esa época, como una scarecrow o puppet o algo, head all small y hasta casi pointy, te lo juro, gangly limbs more chango-like than ever, suddenly *way* too long sin la hermosa chestnut melena para balance it out, o al menos a distract from my awkward skinniness.

Ay, bendita. Too painful. Let me not go there. Déjame regresar al hospital. Which, as you can see por lo de la pésima experiencia en el Camp Fire Girls camp, I must've been *crazy* to beg to stay overnight in! Anygüey, it must've been Kaiser Permanente. Capaz not the one on Sunset, en el mere mere corazón de Hollywood, where I was born, sino otra sucursal. In the Valley. Bueno, pues they knocked me out, put me under. I remember waking up in the middle of the night. Había un niño negro en la camilla de al lado, kind of whimpering. I could see him through a curtain. No me acuerdo bien; I think maybe he had his appendix out. Anygüey, he kept moaning, y las enfermeras iban y venían, revoloteando a su alrededor. At one point creo recordar que le pusieron una inyección, right into his little round naked nalgas. Right in front of me!

I wasn't really scared, pero I slept fitfully. My mouth ached. Y quizás fue entonces when I developed my plaguelike hatred de las fluorescent lights. I remember the door swinging, open-closed, open-closed. Those ghastly, scary, ceniza-green walls, the dim, vein-blue, flickering lights. En el cuarto. En el pasillo.

Simón, con mis estudiantes, por ejemplo, I'm famous for my ferocious refusal of fluorescence. Just say chale to that, les insto. Siempre les tengo que explicar: just think of me like a vampire. Ni bien entro al aula y *apago* las luces. Oh my God, parezco una diva, pero te juro que it's not that (aunque LITTLE EYE: se ha comprobado científicamente que las fluorescent lights not only rob the body of important vitamins—creo que las B vitamins—but they also promote las arrugas y desde luego, dan un look hungover and washed out a cualquiera). Es que ese sickly glow mortecino y el infernal buzzing intermitente directamente me ponen los little hairs de punta. I can't help it. I blame Mercury. Le tengo in Pisces, in the third house. Y eso, según al menos *tres* diferentes astrólogos profesionales, me hace excesivamente permeable. Hypersensitive to my surroundings and to communications del más ashá, pero . . . esa es otra.

Anygüey, ya para la mañana siguiente my slumber party (for one!) en el hospital was getting old. La boca me dolía un chingo y mi vecinito, el del midnight shot in the bottom, ya no estaba. Sentí un alivio inmenso cuando me recogieron para llevarme a casa. I think los médicos recommended I have only liquids, cold things, soft things, por unos días.

No sé cómo corno pasó, porque mami was super-vigilant about doctors, los remedios, following instructions to the letter y bla bla, pero a few days later I ate dinner en lo de los Hurley. Mom let me. You did *let* me mami, remember? Esto siempre era un thrill, porque la Mrs. Hurley (madre de los cinco Hurley kids, las cuatro niñas—Eileen, Kathleen, Maureen, Colleen—y el Tom) servía manjares estrictamente off-limits in our house. Tipo Wonder Bread, meatloaf, Lucky Charms, Kool-Aid. Todas esas exciting gringo delicias. Bueno, esa noche cenamos mashed potatoes and meatloaf, I think.

Pero a la mitad de la comida, just like the anular de la newlywed protagonista en ese cuento de García Márquez, a sudden rush of hot, salty, wet pero en mi caso en la boca, allí mero en la Irish Catholic family dinner table de los Hurley. Por un momento, como alelada, I had no clue. Pensé, this is what meatloaf feels like, *tastes* like, when it melts! Pero then my mouth filled with blood, a borbotones. Maureen and I held napkins to my lips, bien gingerly al principio y luego we full-on *stuffed* them in. OB-vio, al tiro me tuve que ir corriendo a casa y mamá, horrified de que se hubieran desatado los stitches, me mete en la cama, face up, mouth agape, y mami habla con un dentista, o médico, or the emergency room o que sé sho.

And I remember the luxurious feeling—aunque hay que recalcar que Mom estaba rete pissed off with me (even though she herself had *let* me go)—of allowing myself to sink down into the bedclothes, methodically stroking the pseudosilk binding de la manta as was my wont when I was small, para sosegarme (bueno, a decir verdad . . . I *still* do it, pero esa es otra). Anygüey, I lay there, soñolienta, while mami soaked Lipton teabags, como le había instruido el médico, and then pressed them, bien firmly, against my gushing encías. For hours and hours, o tal parecía, my glamorous, unruffleable mami me atendía: wetting and cooling, placing and pressing y reemplazando esos teabags, to staunch that hemorragia bucal.

One of mami's chief concerns, cuando yo era pequeña, was getting me to sleep. Tuvo que inventar algunos clever techniques, porque yo era una niña asmática y—let's admit it—harto anxiety-ridden. Digamos, neurótica. Coño, directamente una pesada. One of her best inventions surgió porque you know those little teensy dots que se ven if you squeeze your eyes shut, really tight, when you're trying to make yourself fall asleep y para no ver monstruos? They're usually like little floating tangerine pinpricks, casi siempre en un fondo azul marino. Bueno, I badgered the hell out of Mom con eso de los dots. Alegaba que me venían a atacar, que llegarían a rodearme if I closed my eyes.

Mom had to use her best wiles para salir—para *sacarnos*—de esa. After weeks (months?) of me fighting against sleep, todas las noches shrieking, "the dots, the dots!" una noche mami me preguntó: "Well, if you had a little girl who saw dots and was afraid to close her eyes, what would *you* do?" Allí muy calmadamente, y como si nada, le dije a mami que I'd line up the glass milk bottles, all in a row en un low shelf que había en mi cuarto, y que los dots allí entrarían and then we'd put the tops on y ya.

Pues gente, it worked. Unas cuantas noches así, patiently putting out the milk bottles, poniéndoles la tapa y puf! Me gustaría decir no more dots, pero in a way, la realidad is even more satisfying (o más banal . . .). No me acuerdo exactly where or when, capaz en una psychology class en la UC–Santa Cruz, aprendí que *everybody* can see the dots, que son sólo una función de extreme cansancio. I was really disappointed for a little while y tuve que ajustar mis paradigmas; había pensado que los dots were *mine*. Pero I got over it, y ahora I see the dots every once in a while, if I squeeze my eyes shut, y OB-vio no me hacen nada, y sé que no te pueden hacer nada. Y pienso en mamá y en las milk bottles.

Y si bien, como he recalcado en otra parte, mami podía ser aloof y también tenía un mega-temper coupled, irritatingly, with a Scorpio-sulk, y era uptight and strict, OK, directamente mean, en mi adolescencia, tenía su costado casi shockingly (por lo inesperado, quizás) tender. I don't mean for a "mom"; quiero decir, for *her*. It's funny. Mis hermanas no comentan este lado de mami. Maybe they don't remember, maybe they didn't see it, qué sé sho. Pero te juro que right now, a casi cinco años de su muerte, what I remember most about Mom, digo, con máxima nitidez, es este tipo de tender, clever, child-sensitive moment de mi early niñez. Y bueno, también momentos que ilustran su extremely bizarre sentido del humor (pero esa es otra).

Pero anygüey, that night—la noche de la hemorragia bucal—mami *no* quería que me durmiera! Me parecía bien strange, even slightly dangerous. Pero she read to me, all night long—así lo recuerdo—de mis adorados Nancy Drew mystery stories.

Note to self: la próxima vez que te pregunten—como hizo la Marianne en lo del dentista last week—do you have or have you ever had excessive bleeding in your life, recuerda este incidente, muñeca! And the next one too, while you're at it.

❧

Onthou jy, Howard? Do you remember the blood, *our* blood? Me dijiste que sí. You wrote me, el otro día: Yes, I remember it clearly. That, and everything else. He abierto la caja de Pandora, mi diario de 1982 (the Transcript le decíamos, bien portentously, remember?), that fetish-object como los ruby slippers de la mera mera Dorothy. I had it with me all along, como la Dorothy tenía esos slippers. All these years lo he tenido cerca, ese diary, siempre conmigo. But it only occurred to me—o sólo tuve las agallas, qué sé sho—to open it and read it, really *read* it again, por primera vez desde entonces, aquí, ahora. Only here in this Montalvo time tunnel or memory vortex did its heel-tapping magic take effect. So here, now, let me rewind. Let me remind you. Let me tell you, my way.

8 - IV - 82

*I*t is 4:30 a.m. No puedo dormir, and I so love to sleep. Without you, me acurruco como una isla, at the center of my island bed. Siento intensamente los contornos de mi cuerpo. The sheets are too cool.

Your card today. Las fotos que mandaste son tan hermosas. No se me olvida nada, *niks,* nothing. Estudio obsesivamente esa foto, the one of us standing there kissing, devouring each other, in the middle of the street, en New Orleans. And it's a wonder to me now; no es tristeza ni pesadumbre que en esa foto haya vida, otra vida, vidita mía, there was another inside me, with us.

11 - III - 82

*Q*uerido Dicki, I wrote my friend, el Dan Dickison (remember?), I conceived a baby with Howard, con mi Montenegro. In Houston. Pero fíjate que only maybe a week later, en New Orleans, it flooded out rich and darkly, durante tres días. Nuestro calvario. We were *really* rattled, aterrados. Finalmente Howard dijo—bitter chiste, ya lo sé—Poor little bugger gave himself up for Lent.

4 - III - 82

*S*o much comes back to me now, even unbidden. Me acuerdo de todo. De todo lo que hablamos, vimos, vivimos. Tengo miedo. No quiero necesitarte. Not you or anyone. Aun con toda esta sangre, know this: I *can* shoulder it as my own brief milagro y pérdida. Y sin embargo reconozco—I *know*—que estamos vinculados, irrevocably joined in this undeniable venture: our future life together in your land.

8-III-82

*H*oward, ha comenzado la sangre de nuevo. Rich, repentino flow, again, y tú tan lejos. I am angry and scared. No entiendo el íntimo funcionamiento de mi cuerpo, este su horario irracional. Doctor tomorrow, de nuevo.

Te escribo a ti, I write *about* you and yet you are also a touchstone, somehow, for so many other things, cosas que siempre he querido decir, y no he sabido cómo ni a quién.

28-III-82

I want to ask: Have you gotten the letter with all the Chinese fortunes clipped together? Quiero saber, exactamente, qué me dices; what is your response to all these words?

Me preguntas sobre la sangre. This is now the *third* issuing of blood in a month. El médico me explicó que después de un miscarriage my cycle may take several months to right itself. But I say to you: La respuesta es otra. Me es obvio que este crazily timed, violent blood flow responde a otro calendario. This hormonal anarchy me alegoriza la vida, and so I'm not worried. Montenegro, my love, es sencillo: you have deregulated me.

❦

You remembered. Oh, you remembered *for* me—pues este sangriento recuerdo lay submerged, en mi inconsciente, cual *rooi, rooi* iceberg— for us, todos estos años. And now, I am remembering *with* you. Abrí la caja de Pandora, I clicked my heels here in this Montalvo Emerald Forest y los ruby slippers de estas páginas me transportaron patrás, back to San Francisco, to New Orleans. Back to you. Estas diary pages, *with* me all this time, todos estos años this memory, esta sangre, sealed between the beige, paper-bag-looking covers de este fat Chinese cuaderno, bought somewhere along the 30-Stockton bus route, on my way home from Berkeley, hacia Chestnut Street, *onthou jy? Non ti scordar.*

Here in these sheltering and exposing green mansions lo abrí y leí. Leí de la sangre, our blood/loss, y te juro, Howard, era como el so-called New World. Like a discovery, uncannily, rather than a retrieval, a re-membering. So unfathomable, ultimately, los funcionamientos de la memoria. Demasiado wounding, esa pérdida, even for me, me and my prodigious memoria de elefante. Couldn't hold on to it. Especially, me atrevo a pensar, after letting you go. La sangre, literal y metafórica, then and now. The blood jet a synecdoche for the uncomfortable yet unavoidable closeness to surface de mi siempre too-ripe, Aztec, persimmon-lush corazón.

There's *all* kinds of reasons for this, OB-vio. OJO: no tengo la culpa. Mi astróloga, la Joanna W., me dice que in my natal chart, Uranus está a sólo seis grados de mi luna en Leo. This proximity promotes extreme hypersensitivity e intensidad. I cannot slow the throbbing pulse, staunch the blood flow at will. Trust me, lo he intentado. Lo intento. Te juro que intento dosificarme. And I *am* getting better at it (at least I *think* I am). Que yoga y Pilates por acá, interval-training health walks por allá. Aromatherapy, breath-slowing machines y masajes all over the show.

Pero mi naturaleza es sangrante (que no sangrona, hey?). Blood expresses me. Y de vez en cuando, it manifests itself, surges forth, breaking through the too-permeable surface. And it goes on way too long, emblema de una herida y símbolo de mi stubborn, unstaunchable, excessive corazón.

XVIII

Currawong Crónica

9 julio 2006
Magnetic Island (Queensland), Australia

Para S.

Te tengo que escribir mi sueño. A pesar de los cries—penetrantes, ghostly, badgering o hechizantes—de los pájaros, some of which seem to go on and on, far into the night (y uno de los cuales me despertó por un momento anoche, around 3 a.m.: an electrifying, piercing, mournful, downward-falling wail que me hizo pensar en el último plaintive, beyond-hope cry de Rima, when the Indians were burning down her tree with her *in* it, en la novela *Green Mansions*), I sleep well here.

Duermo profundamente and I wake at first light, or even before, con los primeros llamados de los pájaros del alba: el *too-whee* y *cha-caw, cha-caw,* luego un uncannily pavorreal-mimicking chillido. Todos esos cries pertenecen al enormous currawong. El *wheeeeee-uh* del pop-eyed, nocturnal curlew. Estoy aprendiendo, en persona (well, OK, *in persona avis*), hasta la famosa risa del kookaburra. Can you believe it? Es así:

ooh-ooh-ooh-uh-ah-ah-ah-ah. Semejante al haunted laugh de un hombre *muuuuy* grande. Like, por ejemplo, el Herman Munster. O mejor, como si riera (as if!) el Lurch, on *The Addams Family*. Remember? Can you hear it?

I had a long dream. Close to morning it all came together, nítidamente y en secuencia. Lo recordé — lo recuerdo — todo. En absoluta, fotográfica precisión. Por eso me he quedado on dry land today. Aunque siempre me ha llamado la atención el coral (OK, OK, more as jewelry, lo admito), tú sabes que me *aterra* el solo pensamiento de un shark. Almost as much as los osos. But I think it was more the human-tiburones I had no desire to consort with today. Por eso I encouraged Pierre y el Paulie to go on that snorkeling trip sin mí. Al Great Barrier Reef. Alegué — and it's true — que el friggin' diurético me hace demasiado sun-sensitive como para pasar ocho horas a la merced del southern hemisphere sun, tan cerca del Tropic of Capricorn y todo, leche solar SPF 45 no obstante. Alegué — bueno, it's actually true — que como me había comenzado la rule (a deshora, just like last August on Robben Island, remember? When that Sangoma in our tour group me hizo comenzar la sangre? What *is* it about my lunar rhythms y el Sur?), I was mortally terrified que la presencia de la sangre would attract an underwater predator. Como por ejemplo un great white. Well it *could*, ¿qué no?

Pero más que nada lo que anhelaba, lo que se me antojaba como un perfect day, era la absoluta soledad. Alone time en un lugar comfy pero extraño a la vez.

For some reason, quería reproducir algo así como el aloneness que había sentido en Cullinan. On the diamond mine. When I first pitched up in South Africa. Pero without the grinding resentimiento. Sin esa horrenda frustración, the dawning sospecha que I'd given my love to someone unavailable, somehow. Someone who didn't have the wherewithal (le faltaba algo fundamental: algo a modo de las herramientas, the skill, la precisión y la pasión, OB-vio) to take the full measure of me in that country. En ese su país. Apartheid. South Africa. Someone who didn't even know what (or how *much* of me) he was missing. Or so it seemed to me, entonces.

Todos los días Howard, my true love, went off, con su university degree en mining engineering, con su solid conocimiento telúrico. Y me dejaba en casa. Literally, waving goodbye desde el umbral, me veo en mi pink Norma Kamali skirt, my teensy, grommeted black tank top, standing forlorn and lonely and foreign en la puerta de ese tiny miner's cottage. Sola todo el día. No TV (como si la tele jamás me hubiera gustado . . .), cero amigos. Curling my bare, tanned toes in the pale-red dust outside. Waiting. Waiting for my love. Howard se iba y venía de mí, a diario, y me dejaba, cada vez más, tierra incógnita. O al menos, that was the narrative I constructed for myself—about him, about us—en esos días.

Y dentro de mí el llanto y la rabia y el conocimiento de mi error—de mi largo, irreversible pilgrimage errado—se me subieron a la garganta. Se virtieron, corrosive, en las páginas de mi giraffe-print-covered diary. Hot, bitter, resentful lágrimas vertí en ese diario. Going-away gift de mamá y Daddy.

But why am I remembering this, telling you this *now*? About Howard and me? About my miserable stay in an Afrikaner diamond-mining dorp? Al menos it was pretty brief. Against all odds conseguí chambita—one of just three lecturers in Spanish *en todo el país*—en UNISA. I hightailed it to Pretoria, not exactly a cosmopolitan mecca—the capital of Afrikanerdom, of apartheid—ay, pero esa es otra.

Anygüey, I think maybe I'm telling you porque ojalá pudiera rebobinar. You know, rewind, to spare my veinte-algo self toda esa angustia ontológica, erótica. Todo eso que viví tan (too much) a flor de piel. Uf! Sha sé, I'm sounding *really* over-the-top, melodramática, downright 'Tine. And besides—sigh—no se puede (spare her). OB-vio.

So, la yo, la que (sobre)vivió hasta aquí, hasta estas páginas, hasta este Sur, este estar aquí rodeada, this time, no por tierra desértica, africana, sino por este intenso green austral, escribiéndote: esta *yo* ha cambiado el script.

Me siento warm, whole, open to the world. Expectant yet relaxed in my skin. "You are the place where something will happen"; recuerdo esas palabras. De la novela *Burger's Daughter* by Nadine Gordimer. Howard me la regaló. Me la regaló en S.F., before he left for home. Cuando la releí el año pasado, antes de volver a Sudáfrica, it struck me as awkward, dated, demasiado Manichaean, its politics demasiado earnest, predictable, in your face. Pero ay, cuánto me conmovió cuando la leí por primera vez, en esos too-long, expectantes meses de 1982, sick with hepatitis (lovesick with yearning), mis padres hoping against hope I'd change my mind and not go.

Pero that *was* me, then. Y OJITO: así también era el mundo—urgente, peligroso. Apartheid wasn't over, not by a long shot. De hecho, estaba, I'd say, en su momento más crispado. Eight long years before Mandela's release. Y eso no era entonces, ni lejos, not even a dream.

🦋

Kwa-kwa-kwa, grazna un pájaro, muy cerca de las plantation-style white shutters, abiertas ceiling to floor en esta casa vieja, donde escribo en una gran mesa de caoba, maciza, oscura y pulida. *Ku-wa,* le responde otro, lejos, hacia el lado del mar. *Screee. Too-hoo, too-hoo.*

Sopla una brisa mañanera. No es muy insistente, pero hace frotar las huge, pale gray-green palm fronds, como lijas, but so softly. Their feathery tips intertwine and release. The variegated *massangeana* rustles (oh, ¡cuántas veces te me fracasaste en mi faraway Inland Empire de Califas patio!). A faint, eucalyptus-tinged scent floats toward me; la brisa me hace cosquillas en los tobillos. How odd, the feel of this dry, plant-infused winter breeze against my feet. Heme aquí, sitting by a wall of windows con vista hacia el mar, pero contenida, cocooned por todo este verde.

En mi sueño, I was back on campus. Muchas veces tengo este sueño, como si los parámetros de mi vida fueran los de un recinto universitario. Ugh! *Is* this my life? ¿Cómo en esa novela, *Giles Goat Boy* de John

Barth? Anygüey, era un campus de adeveras, as God commands. Huge, sprawling, mucho ladrillo. Bien old world o al menos, Ivy League–ish. Parecía Harvard. En otras palabras: my dream-version of a perfect campus, alegoría de un perfect world.

I had a large, pale, soft leather handbag. Como de gamuza era. New. Pero en todo el revolú del back to school, I had misplaced it. Me sentí totalmente bereft, perdida sin mi bolso. Como si ese bolso contuviera toda mi vida. Todo lo importante. My belongings, mis secretos.

Intuí que había dejado el bolso en el dining hall de una residencia, where I'd gone to look for you. El dorm era enorme. Un beehive de actividad. Students coming and going, medio jostling each other. Como en un *real* campus. Digo, no como en Pomona, where there are so few, el ambiente tan precious, rarified que casi nunca se ven grandes concentraciones de gente. No me sentía nerviosa ni hostigada. *Nadie me reconocía.* Era ese comforting anonimato I have always loved about a large university. Como Harvard. UCLA. O Berkeley, o Wisconsin.

Bueno, anyway, a pesar de no haberme sentido muy hopeful about its recuperación, my faun-colored handbag was waiting for me en la cafetería. Me la entregó una trabajadora latina, y la abracé, sobbing de puro alivio. And then I went to look for you. Te busqué por toda esa beehive, subiendo y bajando, buscándote entre tanta gente, gente desconocida.

De repente allí estabas. You put your arm out and stopped me, guided me; you pulled me, muy gently pero insistently over the threshhold, into your room. Recuerdo que tu cuarto era grande, y había una luz filtrada, hermosa. You had your own room.

I was standing close to you; nos mirábamos intensamente. No había palabras. Era como si fuera la primera vez que nos veíamos en mucho tiempo. Como si nada, you were rubbing sunscreen all over my face. You were rubbing vigorously, like one does to a child, all over—¡en los ojos, hasta las pestañas! Me reía. *Stop,* te dije. I was afraid you would rub off el Erace concealer que uso, todos los días, on my scar, right by my left eye y sin el cual me siento exposed, unfinished, vulnerable. *Let me,* me dijiste. No importa. You don't need makeup. You're so beautiful.

(En esta parte el sueño overlaps with "la realidad." Digo, con historical accuracy. Every so often I ask you si se me ve la birthmark. Me sacan *tan* de onda las gafas—even my zillion pairs of designer gafas de sol, lovingly RX-ed en el Claremont village por Dave, de Pigale Optical, quien trabajó en el eyewear de *really* famous films like *Chinatown,* ¿te imaginas? And *Risky Business.* Anyway, I'm paranoid que las gafas me borran el concealer. Pero tú siempre me dices: No, no se ve. Maybe una white lie; quizás blinded by love . . . qué sé sho.)

Al terminar esa (un)cover action, entonces me besaste. Era lento y sublime. I felt the contact, todos los contornos. Sentí tus labios en los míos, gentle pressure. Sentí el frágil contacto con tus dientes, touching the inside of your mouth con la punta de la lengua.

And then, no me acuerdo bien if we were lying down or sitting up, facing one another, en tu cama. It was late afternoon. It was us, *exactly* as we are. Quiero decir: I could feel and ascertain, en el sueño, que era real. Todo parecía heightened. I'd say "slow motion," pero no lo era. It was, rather, that I possessed the attentiveness to time and sensation of a waking dream. I remember your hand was on my lower back. It moved caressingly, hypnoticly, firmly. Muy lento. Sólo se desplazaba cosa de one inch. Inch by inch. I was acutely attuned to that very small place, allí, donde me acariciabas.

We had all our clothes on, todavía. They were more or less loose-fitting (como esos olive green pantalones de hombre, from the GAP, pseudo army-navy, que uso; I think I was wearing those). I remember I ran my arm, my hand, up under your shirt. Con la mano derecha te tocaba el flanco, te abrazaba. With my fingertips I could feel your skin, the definiteness of you, warm, present. Con las yemas de los dedos te rocé la piel, sentí el pulso en tu cuello, my fingers skimmed over and paused at your nipple. Taut. Sentí la respiración; it was yours and mine. You drew me toward you, con la mano derecha.

The sun is up now. Frangipani, sun-released, wafts in through these open shutters. Una pequeña mariposa amarilla drifts, pauses near the shockingly purple row of crotons. The fish kite and the hammock stir on the porch, languidly, invitingly.

Esa mano derecha tuya baja. Almost imperceptibly. Slowly, se mueve. Me acaricia la espalda, hace pequeños movimientos circulares hacia las nalgas. You hold my butt, pulling me toward you, onto you. Siento eso, your hand cupping my butt; a la vez mi atención se bifurca, hacia mis dedos, que te acarician el hombro, el antebrazo. Te juro que I *feel* everywhere: where your hand is moving underneath me, holding me, hacia mi sexo; donde mis dedos se mueven en minúsculo vaivén y te acarician el brazo; donde ahora, my lips replace my fingers and contact your upper arm and I taste you. Sutil. Neutral. Un poco salado.

I am poised, just slightly above you. Soft moans escape your half-open mouth. Siento el calor de tu ingle, pressing into me. Our clothes are on, still. No estorba la ropa. Ni nos fijamos. As your hand circles toward, me escucho gemir. I move toward you.

Hay una extraña, oximorónica sensación. Expectant yet satisfied a la vez. There is no idea of reaching, de progreso. Of getting there. Anywhere. We *are* there. Here. Your skin. Cálida, densa. Your hand on me. Humedad. La otra rozándome los labios like you do, drawing my face toward yours. Tus labios reconociéndome los contornos. No hay noción de urgencia. El tiempo es nuestro. Tiemblo de placer, de anticipación, de presencia. I feel you here with me. Somos, es ahora.

XIX

Por Montalvo Crónica

7 May 2008
Saratoga, CA

Para José "C-2" Cartagena-Calderón

Al subir la cuesta—pretty steep—desde mi "live-work studio" hasta los otros estudios, I pass green, slender-stalked sorts of clumps, topped with yellow, miniature orchid-looking flores. Some get fairly tall—about three or four feet—y despiden un olor dulce, pero no cloying. Algo más cercano al flowering plum (that delicious, damp masa harina smell!), por ejemplo, que a los "Tim Miller." Así le digo a ese pink jasmine, Chilean, I think, con el overwhelming, mega-empalagoso scent, que me regaló Tim de su jardín a couple of years ago.

Ahora subo hacia la cima. Paso el glass-walled cube de la escultora tejana, Nilea. Ella hizo unos pronunciamientos on the edge of annoying en la primera comida. Against Califas. Nació en Arkansas, vivió cosa de diez años, I think, en New York, y ahora vive en Austin, Texas. Oh, nothing outrageous or alarming, la verdad. You know, just los usual stereotypes about California. Pero EYE: anoche en el communal dinner, la Nilea me enseñó a usar un corkscrew normal, as God commands (instead of my wobbly, weird, Japanese Ah-So, con los two little prongs you have to sort of wiggle in entre el corcho y la botella, y que fracasa about 50 percent of the time). Descorché, o como corno se diga, not one but *two* wine bottles, in rapid succession. *And,* plus, she complimented my periwinkle eye pencil de Sephora. So, cómo que le voy a cut some slackecito, ¿no? En cuanto a su casi-critique of Califas.

Más arriba de lo de Nilea [*interruptus*: how bizarre, my lingua franca de los diarios— desde Buenos Aires? even before?—es el castellano. O esa mezcolanza mía. Mientras que antes, my diary from 1982, was *really* English dominant. Did it depend on the interlocutor(s)? I was writing to Howard, then. No sé. Creo que now it doesn't, so much. Strange . . .], on both sides, están tres otros estudios. Each more hideous and bunkerlike than the next. Thank God no me hospedaron in one of these.

Subo la cuesta, behind el bunker no. 61, hacia la mera cima. There's a wooden fence, some scrubby bushes y más de aquellos tiny faux-orchid, yellow-blossomed bushes. The skyline es una pine-topped ridge. Y más acá, a stand of huge, stringybark eucalyptus. Miro hacia las copas de los eucaliptos más cercanos, where I heard a definite raptor calling repeatedly, ayer. Pero hoy nada.

There's a dense, low, grassy scent on the breeze. Es un olor que asocio con los meadow walks que hacía con Nick Vidnovic, through the most secret, remote parts of the UC–Santa Cruz campus. We'd lie naked, soñolientos, al sol, y me daba miedo de que nos aplastaran las vacas que pastaban in those hills. Los sonidos del español carry over to me de repente, brisa-borne, across a small ridge. Beyond, hay una casa, con todos los yuppie trappings: satellite dish, SUV. Latino day laborers calling to each other. Tan cerca estoy, I marvel, de todo lo conocido, familiar, hasta anodino. Pero as I look down from this apex onto the wood-slatted roof and Mondrian-colored walls del minúscule though architect-designed cube where I cloister myself, absolutely alone, six, seven, ten hours a day (podría eloquecer, musito, if not for the glass walls, the ever-whispering green mansions always just beyond), sé que *nada* es normal ni cotidiano.

Como en un sueño—ensueño—I've passed through the looking glass. Estoy transportada a un lugar tan *otro,* my senses on edge. Todo es agudo. In fact, el silencio es sólo una primera—y falsa—impresión. Leaves rustle imperceptibly but constantly. Hay pájaros carpinteros haciendo ese hollow, lightning-fast *tac tac tac,* y bluejays (estos *siempre* me han sacado de onda, can't explain exactly why). And urracas. They remind me, always, de esa película francesa, about that young slip of a girl que tuvo que casarse, against her will, con un dour, hulking, pale-eyed, red-haired, medieval king. Or knight, algo así. No me puedo acordar del título, and it's driving me crazy. Something made me think it was *Beatrice,* pero Pierre lo buscó en el Internido, y rien de rien. Pero anygüey, al final de la movie, no me acuerdo si la chica se suicida, if she drinks some kind of poison elixir and dies. Pa' escaparse del horror de su marido. Or, OMG, ahora creo que era su papá. Pero for sure, tenía una *pet* urraca. Can you imagine? So desde entonces, I've always wanted to try that, pero la verdad, las aves are not exactly mi taza de té. *Especially* a big old crow. Uf! Los claws, beaks y sus beady eyes me dan los creeps, in a way.

Hay cicadas (bueno, esperemos que no sean rattlers . . .), doves, squirrels y lagartos scurrying in the dry underbrush. Hay robins y whip-poor-wills. Halcones. And lurking—según los warning signs amarillos que abundan ahora, y según el faux Steve Earle—siempre la amenaza de un mountain lion. Or even *worse,* de un oso. La amenaza, according to David Washburn, uno de los fellows, is as remote as a lightning strike. Pero, ¿y qué, David? It's out there—*they're* out there—y debo estar, por consiguiente, siempre en alerta.

Ahora vine por el Creek Trail cuesta arriba, hacia la villa. No cougar sightings, which is a damn good thing, porque dejé mi enorme self-defense rock en casa. Eso sí, vine cantando, somewhat loudly, como me aconsejó mi hermana Wiggue. Lo único que se me ocurrió era esa line de la canción de Silvio Rodríguez, from decades ago, "nadie se va a morir, menos ahora . . . ," which I found bizarrely apropos. I'm still not really going fast enough como para work up a sweat, like I'm supposed to, según el Dr. Scott. But today I'm looking, really seeing intently, escuchando, olfateando. I see the great pile of stringybark shavings (no sé cómo llamarlos) around the base of a huge eucalyptus. Miro parriba y los veo en varias fases de moulting, como de una gigantesca serpiente. Como si estuviera, again, en la Isla Magnética.

Eucalyptus pods scattered everywhere, como en esos sweat-drenched, mota-hazed motorbike rides en Santa Cruz, en la secundaria, con el Bob Salter. Extraño, how I once wrote that this scent was, a la vez, medicinal and erotic. Lo de "erotic" sería por los laid-back surfer encantos del Bob. Porque upon reflection, el olor se asemeja, más bien, al de cat pee, ¿qué no? Y déjame no pensar demasiado en qué género de gato . . .

Everywhere, everywhere, me persigue el bewitching olor de esas florcitas amarillas. Está en el viento, even when the bushes are nowhere in sight. Now, bajando de la jodida, nalga-challenging staircase—el so-called poet's walk—behind the villa, a sage, purple candy scent. Ah, the ever-elusive *7e Sens*. Mi grial sagrado, my Golden Fleece. Todo aquí en el Montalvo remite, in a strange way, a los años '80. A San Francisco. Esos meses antes de mudarme a South Africa. Cuando ansiaba estar con Howard, comenzar lo que creía iba a ser mi REAL LIFE. Those bittersweet months when I knew, also, that I'd be leaving la que había sido *tan* mi ciudad, and I needed to burn it into my memory: todo lo que significaba mi San Francisco.

Hay romero. Pero what *is* this green-y, purple candy smell? Porque las pyracantha y romero bushes que abundan ni modo hacen este perfume. Glicinas cover the villa. They're frilly and Baroque and gorgeous, pero they have no scent. Me remiten a la Lucy War (she's jubilating this month from UC–Irvine, oh my God!) cuando me dio a leer *Las ceremonias de verano* de Marta Traba. En esa novela was where I first learned the word "glicinas." Which has now, by the way, pushed the English word for this insistent, hardy, pale lavender-flowered southern vine clean out of my head! *Typical*, no such thing as a "perfect bilingüe," hey?

Ahora cruzo el umbral al Formal Garden. I enter through gates bearing the reminder sign to close them, pa' que no entren los deer que abundan por aquí. I rationalize thus: si por acá no pueden entrar los ciervos, pos tanto *menos* un mountain lion, right? A fin de cuentas, it's the deer they're really after. Solemn, perfectly spaced cipreses line the stone walkway, interspersed with citrus in bloom. ¿Azahar? ¿Alelí? Whatever it's called, es heavenly. El primer día entré por aquí, pero por temor al you-know-what no me atreví a penetrar hasta el fondo, en pos del so-called Lovers' Temple. Quizás encuentre, at last, at last, my own secret garden.

One last look skyward, antes de entrar. Ah, los eucaliptos que bordean el jardín son tan y tan altos. Slender pero *altísimos* troncos. No sé medir bien en números, ni en pies ni en metros. Must be eighty, one hundred feet tall. Al menos. Way taller than the ones in Claramonte. As if they were thriving prodigiously like this porque they really belong here, mejor que en el sur de Califas. Pero eso no tiene sentido (and anygüey, el Paulie recalcaría que son indigenous *only* to Australia). O sea, ni en el norte ni en el sur, as far as Califas is concerned. Pero ni modo. Antes de ir a Australia, en 2006, el eucalipto era para mí un emblema, *sine qua non,* de mi California. Y a veces, even knowing better (y sin confesarlo nunca al Paulie, OB-vio), it *still* is.

OK, gente. Estoy por salir del Formal Garden. ¡Vaya desilusión! I walked down this stone-clad path, hacia una especie de pabellón, which looked bien promising a la distancia. Había un large marble formation, I theorized maybe a sort of shrine para los enamorados. To my surprise and horror, al llegar vi que eran cuatro vatos, o semi-vatos, sort of like satyrs. I mean four torsos and large, pendejo-grinning heads posed around y como si sosteniendo en alto una especie de cisterna. ¡Chale! Esto no puede ser el Love Shack, surely? I continue on, y la cosa pinta mejor. De repente—y con una incongruencia total—I'm off the stone and marble y hay tiny pebbles creating a footpath that leads through *definitely* Australian topografía: cycads, succulents, and Cousin It trees, como los que bauticé así near Uluru (antaño Ayers Rock, pero that was in colonialist-speak) and Katja Tuta.

Justo a la entrada de un grotto misterioso (this *must* be it, I crow triun-
fante, pa' mis adentros), a small, circular stand of odd, skinny, extra-
terrestre cacti and dracaena, y otros weird, harsh, pointy-leaved, spooky
shrubs. Presentan un aspecto amenazante; surely this is the perfect objective correlative, the fortress that inmures a zealously guarded heart.
How cunning, los jardineros! I inch gingerly past the Southwestern for-
taleza y . . . nada. The little pebbled path continues through some in-
sipid, low, purple-budded bushes y termina, just like that, around fifty
feet beyond, en un chain-link fence. ¡Qué estafa! Tendré que mirar el
mapa, look for number eight again (my lucky number, conste, pero you
know that already), el número que corresponde al Lovers' Temple.
Maybe these two plain, parallel stone benches are the spot meant to in-
spire lovers' confidences? Pero they're way too far apart, and uncomfy as
hell. Templo, my nalga!

Wing-fallenly, I make my way back to the gate. Which, pierde cuidao,
I'll mos def close against intruders, whether cloven-hooved or paw-
footed. Y lo del secret garden persiste . . . una asignatura pendiente.
(Casi) mejor buscar que encontrar anygüey, ¿qué no?

XX

Alchemy Armisteadiana
Crónica

27 September / 10 November 2007
Claremont and Davis, Califas

For Samuel G. Armistead, mi padrino

Still too hot, even on this early fall day, para que cualquier cosa, *any* daydream, memory, sensación placentera—y ni modo los supposed endorphins—me ocurra aquí, hoy, as I slog along on my three-mile-interval-training, blood-pressure-lowering, grasa-trimming health walk. Uf, qué flojera.

Aquí en este sendero al pie de (¿en la falda de, se dice?) las montañas San Gabriel. A la izquierda, chaparral still slightly charred from the wildfires hace ya cuatro años y al ladito mero del trail, esos tiny young trees droop. Their long, white, dandelion-puff blossoms appeared briefly en la primavera del año pasado—triumphant, thrust skyward, shockingly phalluslike. The verga trees, les decíamos, Wim and I, when I forced him along on the health walks el año pasado, on his first visit to Califas from South Africa. Pero ahora están marchitos, the small, ex-green leaves and blossom-sarcophagi alike: crinkly, fragile, brown.

Ya que no way me inducirá esta overheated caminata a ningún *natural* Zen zone, Padrino, comienzo a invocar tu nombre, como mantra, como me enseñó la Marie, in her Prana yoga class. Y a ver qué imágenes, cuáles recuerdos, what words will come to me.

Hmmmm, será verdad, como dijera Derrida, que language = hospitality? Déjame preguntarle al Santo-Amor. ¿No es este uno de sus topics?

Who said remembering was easy, natural? Naaaaah. Para mí, como que hasta da trabajito a veces, coño. Me vienen distintas versiones solapadas, hazy, out of focus. O directamente *no* me vienen. Discuto a veces (OK, a lot) con mis hermanas sobre los recuerdos compartidos. Te juro que es como si habitáramos planetas diferentes. A veces tengo sólo un black hole. I wonder if this ever happens to you?

Memory-work. Ese trendy, semi-social-science-y, theoretical term (o therapy-speak) de repente cobra un sentido literal, ¿no? Maybe *this* is why they say "hacer memoria" en Argentina, a la acción de recordar. They make it active.

Repito, invoco tu nombre, Sam, and I swear I feel myself becoming bionic (y no sólo por haber visto ese premier anoche en la tele—by accident, promise, como que I just sort of dully stumbled onto it—una bien cheesy, low production values remake [is there *anything* else on TV y en el cine these days?] de *The Bionic Woman*). Te juro, debe tener algo que ver con lo tuyo, lo del chemistry set. Pero I'll get to that in a sec. De repente, my feet no longer feel like two lead blocks dragging through cement. Mi cuerpo se agiliza; escucho gorgeous trills and calls everywhere. Tiny lagartijas—glorying in the late-season sunshine that I loathe—skittle drunkenly. De milagro I avoid squishing their sweet little Upward Dog o Cobra cuerpos.

¿Has visto alguna vez un colibrí en reposo? Creo haber visto uno years ago, de niña, en la yarda de atrás de mi Agüela Eunice Chávez, en San

Diego. Pero it's pretty rare. Bueno, hoy ha habido *dos*. Pensé por un momento que eran dendrite-extensions de las ramas secas, tan quedos y casi grises estaban. Kind of like Rima, you know, the bird girl in my beloved W. H. Hudson's *Green Mansions*. Cuando el narrador la ve por primera vez fuera de contexto—digo, outside *their* private, magic, bosque-charged context—en la choza con ese more than slightly creepy "abuelo," el Nuflo. Por poco no la reconoce—casi no la *quiere* reconocer—she's faded, demure, shadowy, quiet, nada más lejos de la iridescent, gossamer-clad, trilling woodsprite que le tiene embelesado. Pero anygüey, in a flash mi gaze biónico registered their hummingbird-ness, their miniscule, still aliveness, todo ese shiny, frenetic, teensy *chirp chirp chirping* green in potential.

Hey, Padrino, aren't my best memories—excepto los recuerdos de Santa Cruz, pero EYE: eso fue un breve hiato in the grand scheme of things, seis años seguidos, I think (*sólo* seis años altogether, pienso ahora, fue lo que viví en ese surf- and redwood- and mota-filled paraíso)—aren't my profoundest memories all about el Interior, como quien dice? How bizarre, qué ridículo. Digo detestar el calor, este unnatural blast fur-nace, pero what were, after all, the San Fernando Valley de mi infancia, Madrith, o Pretoria, South Africa, sino otros avatares—precursores—de este, my longest stint ever, so far from my supposedly beloved and yearned-for Pacific?

These are the words, las imágenes, the voices that come to me. I hear them; a veces I can't tell if it's you talking to me, or Daddy. Me descon-cierta. No me asusta. Me adentro cada vez más en mis voces; no siento el contacto, ya, de mis heavily Chung Shi–clad feet con la tierra; the heat-shimmering trailside chaparral is a blur. Podría estar en cualquier parte, sólo escuchando. Bring on the memories. Bring it.

No me importa que sean versiones, sólo versiones. Que haya fragmen-tos, gaps. Es lo único que tenemos, really, if you think about it, ¿qué no? Lo más importante. A lifetime spent searching out, honoring, re-cording minute differences. Versiones. This is mine, for you.

OJITO: you didn't think you were gonna escape sin siquiera un little teensy asadito, did you? Not so fast, not so *fast,* como dijera el Wizard of Oz a la aterrada Dorothy. A verrrr, I *could* tell about:

The Chemistry Set Blowup Caper

Remember the chemistry-set accident when you were, ay, no me acuerdo bien, about nine years old? Hay muchos twists, y la verdad de ese caper me es algo murky. Mi hermana Sarita alega que papá used to tell us how you would take out your glass eye, digo, el standard-issue eye, y metías en su lugar a bizarre-colored one, pa' friquear a la gente (¿ves? Por eso mi vino esa onda biónica). Pero I can't vouch for that. Como que no me acuerdo bien, y mi papá exageraba—OK, directamente *mentía* mucho—I guess you could say. Or, there's the . . .

Visita del Más Ashá Caper

This one you told my sister Sarita about the night Dad died. Te llamaron, la mañana que murió mi papá, el 23 de marzo de 1989, to let you know he was gone. Y le contaste a Sarita que a pesar de no ser una persona "at all spiritual," te habías despertado en la noche, o a primera hora, and my dad was there with you in the room. Ay, Padrino. Ojalá y mi hermana no me hubiera contado de ese caper, just a few weeks ago. Dizque para ayudarme a in-chicken esta croniquita. Porque ¿cómo es que mi papá se despidió de ti con una visita, and not me? Pero bueno, anygüey, we can catch up about *that* later. What about the . . .

Neophytes en Marruecos Caper

You and Dad, novice folkloristas en Marruecos, used to flip a coin or hiss at each other, "You call her, Joe. No, come on, *you* call her, Sam," tal era la inexperiencia—believe it or not, you got *so* damn famous, después—de Uds. dos entonces, para llamar y hacer contacto con los "native informants" who would eventually sing their hearts out, filling with romances sefardíes the mysterious tapes que Uds. desglosarían, juntos o solos, talking into the night, por teléfono, *every* night: partners in crime, in work y en la vida, for over thirty years.

En fin, cada uno de estos capers merece su propia crónica. Pero, ¿sabes qué? I'm kinda reticent, un little hair withholding (por algo tengo a mi Aries sun en la fourth house, ruled by hermetic Cancer). So . . . que se queden con las ganas, ¿no? For now sólo esto, just a little shmear.

XXI

Tuberose Frenesí Crónica

12 junio 2008
Saratoga, CA

For Mary "Cronopia" Raz

Pasé un día bien enJOY intentando escapar el again-blistering heat con la Cronopia Raz, who decided to jugar al ganchito from her work-related seminar en el hotel St. Francis. Desafortunadamente, it was 88 degrees, even in San Francisco, con el resultado de que hasta agarré un slight sunburn on my upper back! Llevaba uno de esos sexy, semi-plunging, wide-strapped tank tops de Anthropologie, y no me había echado sunscreen porque supuse que OB-vio, San Francisco—for sure I'd keep my jacket on.

Anygüey, el *Carnal Flower* de Frédéric Malle (bueno, Dominique Ropion es el perfumer, in actual fact) es, sencishamente, one of the most brilliant perfumes I've *ever* experienced. El libro *Perfumes: la Guía* didn't fully do justicia to just how sublime it is (aunque sí le dan cuatro estreshas). Fuimos a Barneys New York, which was totally beYOND, *much* more akin to the service orientation y a ese feeling de uncrowded, hushed misterio que Macy's y Bullock's y I. Magnin tenían once upon a time. A la Cronopia se le abalanzó este kind of pallid, New Englandish gringo feliz (duh) *oke,* whereas I was swooped upon by two *wildly* queeneriles, jóvenes Latinos! How perfectly apropos! El suyo le agarró la onda right away; le mostraba los more restrained, light florals que ella prefiere, such as *Mimosa* by l'Artisan.

Más tarde, al salir a la calle después de un quick whirl por el cosmetics floor de Needless Markup, la Cronopia unthinkingly doused herself with Serge Lutens's *Araby,* atraída, I suppose, por el nombre. Nos produjo un initial sense of mutual horror, as if she'd stumbled into a Moroccan spice market, o hasta peor, someone's Tunisian kitchen, y encima con un cloying caramel dollop overlay. Ugh. Chale. Pero, as it began to dry down, thank God, and entirely unexpectedly, le comenzó a medio fascinar! Tuve que confesar que me too, and so did this friendly but bizarrely fleece-wearing *oke*—por su provenance del Richmond neighborhood, he told us, although it made *no* sense at all bajo el despiadado sol in Union Square—que caminaba detrás de nosotras. Smells *nice,* girls, nos dijo approvingly. (Me parece que nos había escuchado, conferring about the suddenly pleasant turn *Araby* was taking.) Well, nos hicimos spray prácticamente todo un fragrance department, we told him, pero thanks.

Anygüey, pero earlier, en Barneys, el salesman de la Cronopia le dijo que she likes the kind of fragancia that says come here, and then . . . STOP! I ended up with Miguel, Spanish-speaking, aunque le faltaba algun léxico perfumeril crucial. He did not come up w/ any cute metáforas para sintetizar mi gusto, por ejemplo, pero ni modo. It was clear he "got" me. Y además, I went directly up to him y declaré: Quiero probar *Flor Carnal.* Primero lo hizo spray, on a little card. One whiff sólo de eso, and I had giddy, insanely high hopes. Entonces me lo rocié, just on one spot, in the crook of my right elbow. Well, no lo van a creer. Es, definitely, nardo, pero *cero* empalagoso. Ni siquiera, really, does it hit you over the head with its flowerness. With anything. Al contrario. Un oscuro, rubber, plantlike . . . fleshy effect es lo primero que te da. Y el "brilliance" que describe Luca Turin *is* there. No me parecía appropriate esa palabra al principio, pero creo que it refers to the jasmine, que a veces (sobre todo if you just sniff a bottle of jasmine absolute, alone) huele un pelín a cat pee.

I wore it on and on, mientras el tal Miguel me dio a probar otros Frédéric Malle scents. There is this chévere *Vetiver* one, y un par de otros también pretty nice. Pero *Carnal Flower* was simply *it*. Right from the get-go. Nunca pasó al dreaded efecto Desenex, or to *any* kind of powder. Tampoco se volvió conventionally Oriental on me either, a pesar de la aserción de Luca Turin de que su drydown se asemeja al de *Byzance* by Rochas or Givenchy's *Ysatis* (which L.T. enJOYs but I do not). I couldn't disagree more. No detecto nada de vainilla ni powder ni Desenex, all warning signs a scent is essentially deeply *wrong* for me. InDEED (*pace* Omar on *The Wire*: remember, Santo-Amor; remember, Wiggue?), on me, *CF* se mantiene verde, telúrico, rapturously intense, never cloying, hora tras hora! It is *still* on me, y son pasadas las 9 p.m. I sprayed it on myself tipo el mediodía.

LITTLE EYE: por si todo esto fuera poco, hasta tiene algo levemente reminiscent of . . . guess what, simón, *7e Sens*! ¡Te lo juro (or, I *promise you*, como dijera Howard)! More than perhaps *any* other perfume I've sniffed since *7e Sens's* demise. Bueno, angüey, it is *definitely* of that ilk. Dark, slightly peligroso, aunque kind of classy también, y strange. Especially captivating is its refusal to fade, or become muted—or mutated—en el drydown, and its sharp, poignant persistencia de jazmín. I am enraptured.

La Cronopia me invitó a almorzar arriba, in the Needless Markup rotunda, where we were surrounded by extreme WEALTH. Principalmente las ladies que almuerzan. A charming couple of older women were next to us on one side. Una anciana (literally, parecía tener around eighty or ninety años, en serio), teeny and trim and adorably kitted out en un designer pantsuit y enormes gafas de sol, who sounded like she was from Connecticut (según la Cronopia), rememoraba, con su amiga, un vato bien good looking de su juventud! Del otro lado perched a (trout) blonde duo, mucho más convencionales, una de ellas covered in diamonds, huge as huevos. Surgery and "buttery-blonde" reflejos abundaban; the quiet hum of so much money lulled y desconcertaba, a la vez. A tall, whippet-thin house model (una tranny, estoy convencida), levemente parecida a Janice Dickinson (de antaño), wearing a DUL St. John knit skirt suit, entró y desfiló ante los comensales, attempting to ensnare shoppers into some post-almuerzo Benjy-dropping.

After luncheon, vitrineamos un poco por Union Square, under the incongruously blazing sun. Le conté a la Mary about Jacqueline's, esa old-fashioned perfumería—its name just suddenly popped into my head, como me pasa en estos días, just like what happened with the name *Macassar,* my long-forgotten, fave men's perfume, by Rochas, que dejé con Wim when I left South Africa. Jacqueline's used to be around the Geary side of the St. Francis Hotel. Allí fue donde Pierre me compró el famoso T. LeClerc loose powder, in "Banane," la primera vez que estuvimos juntos en S.F. Pero a couple of years ago buscamos ese shop, and puf, ya no estaba. Like so much of what (and who) was quintessentially S.F. to me. Gone, just gone. Sin dejar rastro.

Anygüey, de repente I looked up, and *there* it was! Todavía en la Geary, pero a couple of blocks away. As if my brújula had shifted, pero just by a hair. How could we have *never* found Jacqueline's again, todos estos años que regresamos a S.F., de visita? OB-vio, la Cronopia and I *had* to go in. And lo and behold, allí había un chingo de heartstoppingly thrilling, dizque vintage, maravishas: *Fidji* by Guy Laroche. *Silences* by Jacomo. Of course *Antaeus, Kouros, Dioressence. Rive Gauche. Yvresse. Ivoire* de Balmain (no *Macassar,* alas . . .). Thank God, el allure-factor estaba en un all-time low, since I'd only *just* gotten my fix (and a mainline at that): *Carnal Flower.*

Le pregunté al gramps salesman (owner, me parecía) how long he'd been at the present location y en un slightly huffy French accent me dijo: ten years. More than twenty years before that, me dijo, they'd been in the St. Francis Hotel location. Le pregunté de algunos de los perfumes, just making conversation, y de repente, kind of out of the blue, looking at a shelf full of Sonias (pero of course, no *Grial Sagrado*), I asked if he remembered Rykiel's *7e Sens.* He shook his head, como melancólico, y entonó, dirgelike: Oh no, no. *Zat's* no more. Zey're not making perfumes like *zat* any more. Zat be-long to a-nozair time . . .

Isn't that absolutely the saddest thing you've ever heard?

Jacqueline's era donde antaño, when I lived in San Francisco, compraba scents que me recordaban Madrith, like *Fidji*. O perfumes que me parecían the epitome of sophistication, peligro, sensuality. Like *Diorella*. O, más bien, *Dioressence. Silences.* Scents I couldn't find in Macy's, even in el Macy's de los early '80s (quiet and swank, not blaring R&B, neon and chrome flashing). Pero now, Jacqueline's parecía . . . a little down en los talones—como su dueño (who, when I asked, by the way, me dijo que había discontinuado los T. LeClerc powders, due to "unreliability of the formulations." Oh the horror, the horror). Como si se encontrara en un slightly unfashionable barrio de Buenos Aires, por ejemplo, en vez de un lugar upscale and sophisticated and MOS DEF primer mundo, like Madrid.

Bueno, fíjate que I still haven't told you un chingo de cosas que quería contar, pero now I've kind of forgotten what it was, or run out of vapor, un poquito. Pero pos, ni modo. Son casi las 10 de la noche; it's *slightly* cooler now, pero, ¿quién sabe what's in store for me mañana? Si quiero trabajar, escribir, tengo que quedarme aquí, here in the terrarium, ¿qué no? Pero no puedo, ni en sueños, subir a la tower, my dream-come-true writing loft, cocooned, cradled aloft, cual crow's nest, rodeada de gently or violently moving hojas. No. En el calor—*anything* above 80 degrees estamos hablando—these windowless glass walls become my architect-designed cárcel, not that osmotic membrana into the green, stirring bosque beyond, hacia el pasado, hacia los recuerdos, hacia mi yo.

Carnal Flower is fading now, pero sólo ever so slightly; a sharp, hasta todavía pungent, jasmine memory lingers. Tal y como el mítico *7e Sens* used to linger, a veces all the way till morning.

Buenas noches.

XXII

Solstice / Shamanic Magia Crónica

21 junio / 2 julio 2008
San Francisco y Saratoga, Califas

Para Luis Vásquez Gómez y Sarita "Eva" Chávez Silverman

Bien podría titularse, this episode, "Pérdida y recuperación del bolso" (*pace* J.C.). El cielo está sólo lightly nublado, pero se siente bochornoso y sopla un African-like zephyr outside. Estoy sentada aquí, en la Mission District de San Francisco, waiting for my charioteer, mi carnal el film studies expert Serge of the Berry. A la izquierda, outside la third-story window de la casa de Luis y María Claudia, amigos de mi hermana Sarita, se ve una loma. The right side covered with piled-close-together casas y el izquierdo pelado. Well, not pelado exactly, máh bien tapizado de ese bleached dun or lomo-de-león colored grass. Dry and crackling as straw ahora, bajo este unnaturally ferocious, unseasonable (*especially* para San Francisco, ¡coño!) sun.

Hay unos low, scrubby trees también. De aquí, even with the laser-precisión de mis RX, trisexual, Prada glasses (OJO: así les digo a los prescription anteojos que te corrigen for close, far, and everything in between), no te puedo decir exactamente what kind of tree it is. Podría ser roble, maybe. Scrub oak. Or acacia. Podríamos estar, exactly, en South Africa, mirando esa loma. So low, dry, lion colored. So near.

Pero ese reverie nostálgico es interrumpido, jarringly, by the voices of two Latino men arguing en español. They're standing just outside a red pickup en la calle, abajo. En la Folsom. ¡Cuánto chillan, joder! Justo que había estado añorando tantísimo volver—en estos too-short two months aquí, patrás en NoCal—volver a vivir en S.F. Uf, just say chale to that, muñeca, pienso. It's only been seven years (or, máh bien: it's *already* been seven years) desde República Arabe Siria 2847, en el Botánico de Palermo, en Buenos Aires (aunque LITTLE EYE: it's been more than twenty desde tus twenty-something San Francisco days . . .). Pero te has desacostumbrado, completely, a big city living. Big time.

Anoche, after the summer solstice fire ceremony en la yarda de atrás de Luis y Mary Cloud (como le dice mi hermana Sarita a la María Claudia), I lay awake at night más de una hora. Bien insólito for me: casi siempre me duermo al tiro, y tranquerilmente. Pero there I was—por el calor casi en pelotas except for an American Apparel, forest green V-neck, tie-dyed T-shirt—en un teensy, casi closet bedroom, overlooking la Folsom Street, unsure if my sleeplessness was caused by the buses and cars whirring by, las intermitentes bocinas, ambulancias, conversaciones callejeras o más bien by the *very* un-S.F.-like still, sweltering, solsticio night.

Te has desacostumbrado a coexistir con los city sounds, musité melancólica y regretfully. And what does that say about you? Como que te socava el street cred as a city girl, as a cooler-than-thou, urban, PoMo flaneuse, ¿qué no?

¡Pero no! Whew. Estos vatos down below no discuten, after all. Oh, they're pumpin' up the volume, alright. Pero nooooo, güey. ¿Si sab's qué? Es como te digo, eso nooooo es verdá. Si te digo ques pura mentiiira, pos. And the other one, su interlocutor, ríe que ríe. Están en pedo (or *hinchos,* como dicen nuestros Colombian hosts) o quizás—more charitably, it's only noon, after all—bien hungover. Puedo bregar con esto, I think. The whirring and whirling and whizzing cars, los chillidos infantiles (¡y no!), sirenas, frenos, backfirings, la brass-heavy ranchy-ranch música blaring de los speakers de los autos que pasan. All this is fading, already, into a blur. Casi imperceptible, already, almost pleasant even. White noise. Like the electric buses que pasaban, regular as relojería, *click click clicking* on their skywires, bajo tu ventana al 2370 de la Chestnut Street, no. 212, right here in S.F. Remember? Oh, remember. *Non ti scordar.*

Estos city sounds eventualmente me hipnotizaban, hasta me reconfortaban. Todos esos entonces-interminables meses, winter and spring of 1982—my countdown to South Africa y yo henchida, ripe with anticipation, escritura diaria y pasión—the 30-Stockton *click clicking* by on Chestnut, en sus riales eléctricos, was my lullaby.

So no worries, como quien dice. You *could* get your city mojo back, mija, como te dijo Pierre. If you needed to. If you wanted to.

Ay, pero I digress. ¡En grande! Todo esto up to here una digresión, in a way. Oh my God. I'm *really* getting bad (um, para variar, máh bien. As if you've ever had *anything* other than a five-track mind—or mouth, ¿no?). ¿Y lo del pelo? I mean, ¿el bolso? My sister Sarita's lost 'n' found purse? And that in itself—if I could ever *get* there—nada menos que una digresión también.

Really, esta croniquita pretendía, I mean, *originally,* narrar de los intense, shamanic skills del Luis, mientras dirigía, last night (con otro über-shaman, peruano), la ceremonia del fuego for the summer solstice. Sigh. Bueno. Pero como esto ya va para larguillo, aquí aprieto. Let me just lance a couple of anécdotas, OK? Para ilustrar los virtuosic poderes de Luis.

Estoy a un solo día de mi exodus del Vortex. Just like when my departure from Buenos Aires was imminent y no podía. No podía no escribir. Pos gente, I'm still hatching like crazy, pero pronto tendré que poner un hasta acá. Turn off la compu and bring it down de esta mi princesa en cahtisho tower, desenchufar y pack it in.

Anygüey, it hit record heat over the past week and weekend (temps 100 and 103, with smoke-filled air, dropping singed eucalyptus hojas, ash, etc.). To escape the antaño green mansions, ahora torture vortex (with no A/C, las temperaturas hit 91 INSIDE; absolutely no cross-ventilation: can you *imagine* how hideous and unhealthy that was? Tried valiantly to pretend I was Mel Gibson, el de antes, OB-vio, de *The Year of Living Dangerously,* por ejemplo, pero it was mos fruitless), me fui con mi hermana Sarita to a fire ceremony in honor of the solstice, con estos amigos de ella, in the Mission District of S.F. Her compadre Luis, colombiano, es un Reiki practitioner and shaman in training!!! La ceremonia *was* New Agey y algo hippie-dippie, pero a lo *Wicker Man* (versión original con Christopher Lee, Edward Woodward y la incomparable Britt Ekland, OB-vio, *not* that abominable 2006 remake, con el egger del Nicolas Jaula!), bien intrigante y moving. Mi hatched former advisee, la Elaine McGlaughlin, living in S.F. este verano, hasta lloró. Anygüey, Sarita y yo pasamos la noche up there el viernes. Pero ni escape ni qué eight rooms: ominously, it wasn't much cooler in S.F. que en el Montalvo—or in L.A., for that matter.

Lo más weird de todos estos semi-apocalyptic signs (el extremo calor, los incendios, the solstice): fíjate que I was stung *twice* en la última semana. First, me picó un bumblebee. Simón, on the left hand, la noche del 18 de junio, as I was trying to climb the spiral staircase al writing loft in the dark, pa' ver si lograba escribir unas paginitas at night, since it was impossible (forbidden to me by Pierre, experto in all things Mac) to turn on the computer de día, por el tema de las temperaturas abnormally high, y eso de que heat rises, y bla bla. Out of nowhere, a big ol', *huge* bumblebee attached itself to my left index finger; sentí un repentino dolor atroz and I looked down, y por poco me caí patrás. Instinctively I shook my hand—it looked like a tiny, fierce, furry creature, te lo juro, un grizzly bear en miniatura clinging to my finger. The horror, the horror. Por suerte mi vecino el Adán Avalos was right there, y me sacó el stinger and we taped it into my diary y todo. Pero the damage was done. Soy recontra allergic. Not anaphylactic or anything, como mi Agüela Chávez, pero *still*. Almost. Anygüey, luego, on Friday night, la mere mere noche del solstice, en esa blazing hot night in S.F., me picó una araña, on the right hand!

Luis, el healer/shaman in training, me interpretó los dos stings. Dijo que lo del bumblebee, *especially* occurring on the eve of Mercurio going direct, era un sign that I'd done enough of the deeply reflective, emotional, memory-based, gathering and creative work (my hatching— after weeks and *weeks* of thinking, remembering, rereading mi diario, ese Transcript, and scribbling en el diario actual—the "Momentos Hemorrágicos Cronica," por ejemplo). The left hand is associated with the heart, con lo creativo, lo femenino y el pasado. I *am* pretty allergic, como dije, y ese sting ached, pulsed, got hot, red, and swollen—and then itched like a mother—durante varios días. Según Luis, ese sting fue un "hasta acá": especie de farewell to the type of work I'd been doing, casi seis semanas, en el Retrete.

Luego la araña, según él, is sacred in African folk traditions (I remembered Anansi, en ese librito I'd gotten for el Juvenil, when he was little). Y la diestra is all about "masculine" energy. Doing, finishing, putting into action. So, I'm hoping to be able to polish and finish these croniquitas. And, with a little luck (or spidey poison?), hasta ponerlas en orden, help them find their place, en lo que me queda de este Retreat, bueno, del verano. Antes de tener que volver a mi day job, OMG.

※

Ay, entre todo esto del extreme calor, y los bodily injuries and potent poisons, se me olvidó, pero *completely,* lo de la pérdida y recuperación del bolso. The tale of my sister Sarita's purse, missing and thought disappeared forever (posiblemente hasta stolen durante la solstice-fest— había un chingo de gente en lo de Luis and Mary Cloud, after all) y luego found, bajo las telephonic ministrations de Luis.

El vato *truly* has the touch, te lo juro. After frantically searching the apartment, un chingo de veces, Sarita called Luis en el trabajo. He basically talked my sister down, justo antes de que ella tuviera que lla-mar a mi nephew, el Nico, to come all the way from Pacific Grove con las spare keys del Prius. Luis walked her through todos los ambientes del flat hasta que reapareció el bolso, just as mysteriously as the way it had gone missing. Simón, gente, allí estaba: kind of tucked all snug into a pile of clothes en el piso de un bedroom, a room she'd searched pa-rriba y pabajo, sin éxito, *several* times already.

Pero anygüey, esa—la del bolso, la de los shamanic, a la distancia rogue purse-whispering poderes de Luis—es otra crónica. Por ahora, let's reflect a bit on esa allegorical interpretation que dio Luis a mis hand wounds: the painful yet mythically superpower-endowing picaduras de bumblebee y araña.

XXIII

(Almost) Milagros Crónica

24 enero 2009
Thompson Creek Trailhead
Claramonte, Califas

For Deborah "B-2" Barker-Benfield

A borbotones vienen las palabras. At last. Después de bastante— demasiado—tiempo. Digo, way too much time, for me. ¿Dos meses? ¿Tres? Well, no ha sido un período fallow, or not *exactly* pues están, of course, mis dreams. Bubbling up, también— con el tarry viscosity and regularity de ese *glug glug glug* que se escucha at the La Brea Tar Pits— from the primeval swamp *sine qua non*: el subconsciente. My dream/ journal. Working on, working *out* tantas cosas.

Howard. Santo-Amor. San Francisco. South Africa. Mis sueños, my *olifant* remembering, writing out my dreams, ay, *tanta* hermosura pan- tanosa. Una hemorragia onírica, we could say. To keep hold of, to honor la imagen de la sangre, my touchstone desde mayo del año pasado. En el Montalvo.

Pero en términos de mi escritura, mis crónicas, nada. *Niks.* Normal, ¿no? I mean, this nothing. This wordlessness (ja ja, as IF. As IF I could *ever* go wordless del todo). Después de haber trabajado tan intensely, so concentrated, desde, digamos, mayo hasta . . . all the way through until the end of October. Hasta entregar el libro, mandarlo a mis Musos, a Raphy. Y hablando de eso, what *can* be taking ese second reader so damn long? Van ya casi tres meses que lo entregué. I know, I know. Que los holidays, que Chrismy, que fin de año y bla bla. Pero el miedo, esta anguhtia, an ever-tightening nudo of fear and apprehension gnawing.

No quisiera ser como la Sally Field, en ese su famoso (y *tan* egger!) Oscars moment: "You like me, you *really* like me." Wish I could be less thin-skinned, not care. Know I'm good no matter what, la escritura, yo, escritora. Pero I can't shake, del todo—no matter que ya escribí y publiqué un libro with legs (según Raphy, según el Paulie, experto Googlero), no matter que gané ese writer-in-residency en el Montalvo last year, no matter *anything*, joder—can't shake la necesidad de saber, this (pathetic, ya lo sé) need for approbation.

¿Quién coño tendrá el condenao librito anygüey? And what do they think about it? ¿Le gustará? ¿Le habrá "llegado," digo, you know, tocado? *Ohhhh, ahhhhhh,* como dijera Al Pacino as Sonny, al John Cazale (Q.E.P.D.) as Sal, in *Dog Day Afternoon*: "I'm *dyin'* in here!"

Confieso, pasando ahora a otro rubro (como dijeran en mi adorado and now oh so far from me Río de la Plata), y hablando de heavy anxiety (my disease, mi maldición), haber estado harboring some little, *teensy,* semi self-loathing pensamientos lately. Not that I've ever had any attachment a la guita, digo, al dinero in and of itself. No desire whatsoever to be rich, sino más bien al contrario—vestiges de mi fervor revolucionario de la secundaria, de la universidad y la graduate school, I reckon. La mera idea, la noción de *auténtico* wealth de hecho me produce una especie de náusea ideológica (yes, still!), ontológica. Incomodidad. Pero on the other hand, confieso también no estar inoculated, not completely, contra los charms de lo que puede *hacer* el dinero. Soy *bien* provider-ish. Tan Mars in Capricorn en la casa dos, so very Saturn in the twelfth house.

Al principio, way back en el fall del 2007, cuando volví de ese epic East
Coast trip—la boda de mi hermana la Wiggue en Nueva York, con el
George, staying en lo del Santo-Amor y su familia in yucky, yuppie
Princeton, sentada hora tras hora en los archives in the gorgeous, Goth,
Princeton library, copiando a mano (I know, ya sé, ¿qué boluda, no?
Pero te juro que I forgot to take el laptop! Típico . . .) de los diaries y
otros papeles "prohibidos" de Alejandra Pizarnik—when I looked at my
statements del retirement, ese IRA que heredé de mamá, me dio un little
frisson of shock. Pero eso fue sólo initially. Later, watching it all sieve
away, more and more, todo el año pasado, despite being with Compak
Asset Management con todo y su famoso pronunciamiento, "Moe
never loses the principal," pos I was kind of numb. Me parecía . . .
¿cómo decirlo? Todo teórico.

Pero ahora, se aproxima el day of reckoning. Hay que hacer los taxes y eso
siempre inplica un cara-cara with all my Type-A record-keeping. Y sé que
voy a descubrir, I mean, *confirmar* lo siguiente: this has been a pretty
fucking historic, prodigious bloodletting. Wouldn't you say? I mean,
worse than anything our parents (our shared Romanian-judío bloodline;
mis elders nuevomexicanos) ever experienced, según dicen los headlines.

Todos están—estamos—jodidos, little eye. No hay quien se escape. Y
sin embargo, siento una especie de stinging resentimiento. No puedo li-
brarme del todo, try as I might, de la idea (burguesa, la neta: I cop to it)
de que I did everything "right" (Daddy estaría orgulloso, creo) y
somehow it's not fair. A la vez, soy consciente de que esas palabras son
absolutamente ridículas.

Let's just put it right out there: $300,000, give or take. Esfumaos. And
it ain't over yet, de eso estate segura, muñeca. So, con estos dark, abys-
mal, swirling thoughts, y bajo un faint, lacy veil of drizzle, comencé el
health walk this morning.

Un primer milagro me encaró, close to the outset. Get this: todos los
teensy, budded tips de la mimosa tree (*acacia*, el Paulie would correct
me, or worse: *wattle*! Yuck, can you imagine? Y creo que hasta it's the
national plant de Australia! How is it possible que le hayan dado un

nombre tan grotescamente guajoloteril? Ay, me muero de risa—or LOL, como dicen ahora), que hace una semana estaban morphing—de closed, emerald-green dots a bolitas de casi-chartreuse—son ahora los quintaesencialmente primaverales puffs de amarillo solar. Hasta comienzan a despedir, even under this doggedly wintry, leaden, low sky, my ür-scent: green, powdery, vaguely anís-like, my homecoming, Santa Cruz, and South Africa scent: ah, mimosa.

But it's too early, *way* too early. Estamos sólo a enero, a fines de enero. Y esto, these yellow sun-puffs, should only burst into bloom around my birthday. Primer día de la primavera boreal, first day of Aries. Oh, qué miracle ni qué eight rooms, as el Serge of the Berry would say. This is an aberration.

Pero little eye, eh? Un definite milagro *sí* hubo. Como para roust me out of this productivity-paranoia y (non!) guita-induced casi ataque de pánico. Oye: have you ever seen raptors flying en manada, o bandada, you know, in a flock o como corno se le llame a un huge group of birds? Son aves solitarias o a la suma, in a pair. Todo el mundo sabe eso. Pero right after ese disconcerting flash of premature amarillo, al costado derecho del trail, I looked up and wheeling, circling slowly, there they were. Algunos negros azabache against cielo plomizo y otros softer, a lighter dove-gray, como si fueran la sombra de los negros: un torbellino de hawks. Sé lo que digo.

Take me, oh take me with you, les imploré, alzando los brazos. Transform me. Al instante, me reconocí infinitamente pendeja y hasta (para variar) algo cursi, en ese semi–Richard Harris in *A Man Called Horse* moment. I mean, pensé pa' mis adentros, ¿qué coño haría yo, with a bunch of feathers on my arms? Pero por un momento la idea de subir, escapar, vanishing into the ether en lo más alto de la ola, fue irresistible.

No more plunging retirement accounts, no más angustiante espera de ese elusive second reader's outstanding reportaje.

Protéjanme, I begged that quicksilver gathering of halcones. Guide me. Y me siguieron, te lo juro. Cada vez que miraba skyward, there they were, right above me. Dipping, circling, stitching the dense clouds, formando un living origami de darting beaks, soaring alas. Cual si cosieran, right there en el cielo, un intrincado, desconstruido design, como un Rei Kawakubo for Comme des Garçons, circa los early '8os.

Sos mi totem, le dije al hawk, pero *what* does it mean, esto de verte en bandada? Can an aberration signify a blessing? Your wings black V's, like cross-stitches, como un airborne alfabeto. Oh, I wish I could read you.

For now, lo único que sé es que el movimiento plural de estas negras alas ha desatado—como por milagro—el deseo, urgent, unstoppable, de la palabra.

XXIV

Todavía Wild (at Heart)
Crónica

21 agosto 2008
Thompson Creek Trail
Claremont, CA

Para Pierre, for our home

OK. Es verdad que you're back home, reintegrándote medio grudg-ingly, medio gratefully, y lejos ya de tu green mansions, cougar-evading, ruby slippers, memory vortex interludio del Montalvo. Simón, gente, patrasito estoy en este suburban college town, en el easternmost edge de L.A. county.

Pero pensándolo de otro modo (menos resignada, menos defeatest) — putting el acento en otra sílaba, por ejemplo — maybe el concepto mismo del *edge* debe ser recalcado. Al filo de. Not wild (no vives *en* los San Gabriels, after all, en una cabañita: uf, somehow hasta la sola ima-gen de eso reminds me of the Unabomber! — con wood-burning stove y todo ese rollo, sino al lado de, right at the feet of, en la falda de), pero ni tame tampoco. Precisamente porque *no* estás en el centro de la ciudad (bueno, as if L.A. even *had* one, pero you know what I mean; the "real" L.A., léase: the Westside) sino al este de. Last outpost, o casi, en la Route 66, antes del puro desierto.

Emblema de este todavía wildness (however compromised, however attenuated, however endangered), acabo de ver un coyote, te lo juro, about three feet from me. Not running, not walking. Un poco como yo iba, ese trickstery southwestern ícono *sine qua non* come to life. Startlingly, undeniably de carne y hueso.

Los escuchaba un chingo en Montalvo, howling en el bosque. Estaban cerca y eran muchos, it seemed. I was glad. Esos coyotes'll give that puma a run for its dinero, pensaba, satisfecha. Los escucho aullar aquí. De cuando en cuando, their howls cut through, rise above the muffled roar de la 210E freeway extension. I can hear them after dark, when the winds change pero la rush hour traffic hasn't died down del todo. Los high-pitched howls drift in, a mournful, choral overlay to the *whoosh whoosh* de la 210, por la ventanita del master bathroom. I shudder sometimes, they sound so close; I sigh with alivio de que las Niñas sean exclusivamente indoor cats.

Pero la civilización encroaches just enough on la barbarie aquí en SoCal suburbia que los coyotes are *not* all that easy to see. Y cuando sí, pos they're usually either dead or you see the back of them, escapándose de un too-close encounter.

Este venía muy canchero, just as casual and cocky as you please, como con un sprightly trotecito. De hecho, took me a moment to recognize him. Digo, como tal. Coyote. El reconocimiento me llegó algo así como el *click* de esas delayed-action cameras. Creo, more than anything, que quedé medio atónita porque cruzaba el health trail bien brazenly, right in front of me, pero leashless. Sin dueño. Y esto—esta condición, estrictamente ilegal en los parks y senderos de Claremont—tipped me off.

Me miró como de reojo, bien furtive and stealthy, just like their rep says they do. Pero no se inmutó. Ni un solo momento. Continuó en su unmarked camino. Cruzó el trail y trotó, steadily, parallel to me unos instantes pero going the opposite way. A dun-colored, terrier-sized bit of furred wildness.

Al pensar un poco (I kept trotting, myself), era casi del mismo tamaño de los tres dingoes que vimos ese día, el del base hike around Uluru (antaño Ayers Rock), remember? Almost exactly two years ago. El día que el Paulie le gritó a ese turista australiano who was celebrating, bien enthusiastically, the improved weather and the opening of the Rock: "It would be *fucked* to climb, don't you know? You shouldn't climb!"

Anyway, tal y como esos tres dingoes hadn't, este coyote no traía nada en la boca tampoco, thank God. Como ellos, trotaba rather purposefully (el propósito invisible a ojos humanos), sus rubios flancos both stitching and unravelling the seam entre lo doméstico y lo salvaje.

Leaning toward the latter, OB-vio. Inclinándose hacia lo wild.

Afterword

Linguistic Perspectives on Code-Switching

Michael Shelton, Occidental College

"Put that *in your pipa and fúmenlo, mijos."*
"Well, it will *warm up on the skin, me dijo."*
"Los estudiantes no tenían idea; quedaron completely perplexed."

What's your reaction to these sentences? How do you feel when you hear people speak like this? Do you find it pretty? Are they examples of broken Spanish or broken English? Examples of how some people just can't stick to one language? Or perhaps the skillful expressions of a fluent bilingual? All of these thoughts are common reactions to what many people know as *Spanglish,* and what linguists refer to as intrasentential code-switching, the alternation of two languages within a single utterance. Interestingly, many people do not object to language shifts between sentences, but switches within the sentence or clausal level often evoke strong emotions. Perhaps this reaction is due to the traditional understanding of code-switching as a manner of compensating for incomplete acquisition of either of two languages. To the outsider, it may appear that these speakers change back and forth between their two languages when they encounter linguistic difficulties. However, contrary to these impressions, research in linguistics over the past few decades has shown that among native code-switchers these apparently random shifts in language are in fact systematic and rule-governed.

One way we know that code-switching is not random in nature is the fact that proficient bilinguals, whether they are code-switchers themselves or not, have intuitions about "good" and "bad" switches. For example, most bilingual speakers of English and Spanish will accept the sentences above, which were extracted from pages of this book. However, these same speakers will reject a switch such as *Me dijo Carlos que ha worked there for two years.* If some switches are deemed acceptable and others not, then there must be some system that informs our judgments. We start to ask ourselves: Where in a sentence is code-switching possible? What makes certain switches sound ungrammatical? Questions such as these have led to a substantial body of research in theoretical linguistics that seeks to identify the grammatical constraints on intrasentential code-switching.

The great majority of code-switching occurs at points in the sentence where the structure of the two languages follows similar patterns. For example, a native code-switcher might say *Estoy muy cansado because I've been studying all day.* This is an acceptable switch, because both the English sentence *I'm very tired because I've been studying all day* and the Spanish sentence *Estoy muy cansado porque llevo todo el día estudiando* divide the sentence into a main clause and a subordinate clause at the same point (between "tired" and "because"). In contrast, we reject an utterance such as *She wants Mark comprar la camisa negra,* because the two languages are incongruent at the point of the switch. In English the second clause of this sentence would contain an infinitive: *She wants Mark* to buy *the black shirt.* The Spanish clause, however, requires the subjunctive: *Ella quiere* que compre *Mark la camisa negra.* This divergence in the syntax of the two languages leads us to consider the sentence an example of a "bad" switch. Another observation that researchers have made is that switching usually does not occur between bound morphemes. We can say *When I called yesterday my wife estaba jugando con los niños,* or *When I called yesterday my wife was playing con los niños,* but not *When I called yesterday my wife was play-ando con los niños.* The "-ing" and "-ando" at the end of words like *playing* and *jugando* are suffixes that are bound to their verbs and thus are inappropriate points for code-switching. It is clear from examples such as these that code-switching is not random in nature. Its systematic use exemplifies the need for high proficiency in both languages involved.

We might also ask ourselves why a person would choose to code-switch in the first place. Wouldn't it just be easier to speak one language? Studies in conversation analysis show that the use of code-switching serves a pragmatic function. Speakers are able to communicate additional information and employ stylistic differences by alternating languages. Take for example the sentences *I can't today, dijo Juan* and *Juan consultó el diccionario, looking for the word he didn't know.* In the first sentence, we see an example of a code-switch that features reported speech. The quotation is spoken in English, and the speaker's own words appear in Spanish. This use of code-switching draws the listener's attention to the difference between what Juan said before and what the speaker is saying now. In the second example, we see another pragmatic tool, the elaboration of previous information. The phrase "looking for the word he didn't know" reveals why Juan needed the dictionary. These discursive strategies are only available to the bilingual community. Switches are also often employed to emphasize certain information, such as in the example *Then we saw this huge guy que pesaría el doble que yo waiting in line at the store.* The shift to Spanish in this sentence cues the listener to more details about the person the speaker saw. Furthermore, sentences such as *Me corté el pelo, did you notice, para la boda de María* and *Pues as a matter of fact lo tengo aquí mismo* illustrate how code-switching appears frequently with parentheticals and formulaic expressions. As we can see, the use of two languages is not simply an alternative to expressing the same information in one language. Rather, it enriches the message with cues to aspects of the sentence the speaker has chosen to highlight. These examples represent how code-switching can be employed by a bilingual speaker for a wide range of conversational strategies.

Another motivation for code-switching is its social value. Despite the fact that the large majority of the world is multilingual, in the United States we tend to see monolingualism as the norm. While our country prides itself on its diversity, both ethnic and linguistic, the majority of the country predominantly speaks only English. This puts highly proficient bilinguals into a small subclass of society. Work in sociolinguistics describes that the standard variety of speech in a community enjoys overt prestige. English is undoubtedly the prestigious language in the United States, as it is the language that we read in national newspapers and hear on the nightly news. Where does that leave speakers of other languages? Those who speak both the prestigious language and another are in a unique situation. They are able to speak the standard with greater society, but they may also use their second speech variety as a marker of social identity. Speaking a particular dialect or language may even be a requirement for acceptance in certain social groups. Among the speakers of nonstandard varieties, a different kind of prestige arises. Spanish holds covert prestige among many U.S. Latinos. The inability to speak Spanish may be interpreted as a lack of cultural pride and may lead to a lack of social acceptance within Latino communities. Thus bilingualism rises as a tool to belong to multiple groups in society, and code-switching emerges among society's most proficient bilinguals. These speakers are able to alternate back and forth between two varieties, not due to questionable competence in either language, but for specific purposes. The mixing of two languages affords them not only stylistic features that a monolingual conversation is incapable of conveying, but also the opportunity to express their identity as a member of two linguistic communities.

While it is clear that code-switching is highly valued among particular social groups, what is its place within the broader context of social interaction? Sociolinguists also ask questions such as: With whom is it appropriate to code-switch? What type of reactions do non-code-switchers have to mixed speech? Research on language attitudes has shown that many of the first impressions we have of others are based on the way people speak. Studies in this area indicate that many people have quite different opinions about an individual's intelligence, helpfulness, friendliness, and other traits based solely on his or her language use. These perceptions have an impact on all of us and the type of lives we lead. Our ability to find jobs, secure housing, and form relationships oftentimes hinges on the first impressions we make on others, impressions that are often based on our linguistic traits.

The question of language attitudes brings us full circle, back to our opening examples. What are your impressions of code-switching now? A substantial body of research has led us to conclude with certainty that code-switching is not an example of broken speech. It is, on the contrary, the skilled use of two linguistic varieties by a highly proficient bilingual. Do you find it pretty and expressive? Or unpleasant and exclusive? These reactions reflect the way society treats distinct varieties of language use in different circumstances. From a linguistic perspective, code-switching represents a fascinating phenomenon that we will continue to study for years to come. It offers us a point of investigation to learn more about the structure of individual languages, as well as the universal qualities of language in general. Similarly, the social facets of language are informed by studies of bilingual language use. Susana Chávez-Silverman's *crónicas* offer us another view into the bilingual mind and the bicultural experience. As we read her witty thoughts, we share humorous and touching moments that can only truly be experienced in two languages. Her second collection is a rich addition to both literature and linguistics alike.

WRITING IN LATINIDAD

Autobiographical Voices of U.S. Latinos/as

SERIES EDITORS

Susana Chávez-Silverman
Paul Allatson
Silvia D. Spitta
Rafael Campo

Killer Crónicas: Bilingual Memories
Susana Chávez-Silverman

Scenes from la Cuenca de Los Angeles y otros Natural Disasters
Susana Chávez-Silverman

Butterfly Boy: Memories of a Chicano Mariposa
Rigoberto González

Madre and I: A Memoir of Our Immigrant Lives
Guillermo Reyes